Sites of Race

In the spirit of Stuart Hall
1932–2014

Sites of Race

Conversations with
Susan Searls Giroux

David Theo Goldberg

polity

First published in 2014 by Polity Press

Polity Press
65 Bridge Street
Cambridge CB2 1UR, UK

Polity Press
350 Main Street
Malden, MA 02148, USA

ISBN-13: 978-0-7456-7178-9
ISBN-13: 978-0-7456-7179-6 (pb)

A catalogue record for this book is available from the British Library.

Typeset in 11 on 14 pt Sabon
by Toppan Best-set Premedia Limited
Printed and bound in Great Britain by T.J. International, Padstow, Cornwall

For further information on Polity, visit our website: www.politybooks.com

Contents

Acknowledgments   vi

Introduction   1
1   Race to modernity   14
2   Global racialities   35
3   Modernity's civic religion   48
4   Racial states   66
5   Fearing Foucault   83
6   The raciologics of militarizing society   108
7   Migrating racisms   130
8   Civic lessons   152
9   Racial (ir)relevance   170
10 Reiteracing Obama   185

References   209

Index   218

Acknowledgments

This book started from a long conversational interview Susan Searls Giroux conducted with David Theo Goldberg in New York City in 2005. A version of that interview was first published by *JAC* in 2006 ("On the State of Race Theory: A Conversation with David Theo Goldberg," *JAC* 26, 1–2: 11–66), and is used here with the kind permission of that journal. Two further conversations, both in Irvine, California, took place in 2007 and 2011. The three conversations, while engaging a broad array of issues and questions, were extensively edited to focus on race and racism for the purposes of this book.

Many have helped us in shaping the book. Henry Giroux pushed us at times to address questions we might otherwise have overlooked. Nisha Kapoor offered an insightful set of responses to our discussion on immigration, the revisions consequently significantly improving chapter 7. Nasrin Rahimieh graciously offered her home and warm hospitality. Noa Reich and Maia Krause did yeoman's work in transcribing the interviews for us. Maia and Claudia Caro Sullivan spared no effort in securing the rights from Cuban artist Alexis Esquivel for the cover image. Anna Finn creatively curated the index under tightly pinched deadlines and with a helpful but less than ideal digital app.

The folks at Polity Press have been delightful to work with. We are especially grateful to our editors Pascal Porcheron and Louise Knight, to our production editor Clare Ansell, and to our copy-editor Justin Dyer. The manuscript has been much improved as a consequence. We thank also a set of anonymous reviewers for the Press whose comments pushed us to clarify some things that otherwise would have remained less lucid.

All books tend to be more collaborative than is often acknowledged. This is especially so with one both produced out of a set of sustained conversations and that would not have materialized but for the engagement with each other over an extensive period. We hope that this spirit of engagement and the passion of critical exchange are reflected in the pages of the book.

Introduction

Susan Searls Giroux

Invited to address a forum hosted by the Liberation Committee for Africa in June 1961, James Baldwin opened with the following remarks:

> Bobby Kennedy recently made me the soul-stirring promise that one day – thirty years, if I'm lucky – I can be President, too. It never entered this boy's mind, I suppose – it has not entered the country's mind yet – that perhaps I wouldn't want to be. And in any case, what really exercises my mind is not this hypothetical day on which some other Negro "first" will become the first Negro President. What I am really curious about is just what kind of country he'll be President of. (2010: 9)

Kennedy's promise would come to fruition not thirty, but nearly fifty years later, and as Baldwin implied, times are indeed tough for America's first black president and for the nation more generally. As this book goes to press, the US remains a house deeply divided, having recently suffered through a government shutdown and repeated threats to default on its credit for the first time in its history, internecine fights to derail implementation of Obamacare, the further slowing down of a fragile recessionary recovery, and all the while lurching from one Middle Eastern and Eastern European conflict to another that threaten to inflame these regions and ignite another wave of global terror.

What the nation long tolerated as the norm for the majority of its black citizens – creeping poverty; high unemployment; depreciating home values; no or minuscule health care, pension plans, and job security; and deplorable schools – has now spread to its once robust and mostly white middle classes. Too many Americans are confronted with the sting of poverty of a particular kind – a poverty that happens suddenly, seemingly without warning, and in the immediate aftermath of a debauched era of riotous, wasteful, and vulgar accumulation of wealth for the very few, while their glittering riches and lavish lifestyles, the very stuff of frenzied media spectacle, fuel the fever-bright fantasies of the rest. Too many, rich and poor alike, have embraced what Achille Mbembe calls "an idealized lifestyle that surrendered unreservedly to the world of things (wealth, luxury, and display)" (2004: 378). And now in the post- (or pre?-)recession morass, they lack the financial means to partake of its enervating pleasures and the intellectual means to imagine another mode of existence. People feel cheated and burn with resentment – a resentment all too readily inflamed by a racist imaginary that links white privation and pain with the phantasm of black ascendancy – apparently made all too real by the ascent of one, or "The One." Indeed, neoconservatives have for decades primed their constituencies for investment in this form of "racial delirium" (Mbembe 2004: 380). By excoriating state concessions to "special interests," implicitly understood to represent "blackness and the interests thought most directly to advance black life," they created – in a time of protracted racial inequality – the strange paranoia of "inverted threat," the panicked anticipation of "a black state" allegedly organized against the interests of maintaining white privilege, power, and control (Goldberg 2009: 337).

What country, indeed, is the US? No one has been more analytically attentive to Baldwin's provocation than the South African-born, cosmopolitan philosopher of race David Theo Goldberg. His body of work has been devoted precisely to historicizing and theorizing the unprecedented damages incurred from nearly four decades of racially driven neoliberal policies that are Barack Obama's inglorious bequest – and a set of crisis conditions only exacerbated by his complicity with, and participation in, the national commitment to willful historical amnesia. The colorblinding imperative that has marked the racial politics of the post-civil rights era both in the US and globally has effectively pre-empted individual and collective capacities to understand the connections between the racist exclusions of the past and the contemporary racially prompted transformation of state apparatuses, of sovereign power, of *raison d'état*, as it shifts from welfare to warfare. The racial fissures that have split US society migrate globally, translate locally, and return with a vengeance – what is "buried, alive" here, Goldberg (2009: ch. 1) reveals, finds fertile soil in a range of geopolitical sites the world over.

We live, thus, in a moment marked by widespread confusion over the meaning and political significance of race both within and outside of the academy. This I tell my students at the beginning of each semester. It is also why each semester in an undergraduate lecture hall or graduate seminar we commence with Goldberg's oeuvre; his innumerable contributions to race theorizing are as bold and capacious in their historical and geopolitical reach as they are exacting and meticulous in their modes of analytical engagement. With the dismantling of institutional, legal segregation in the US and of the formal apparatus of apartheid in South Africa, Goldberg argues that a form of common sense has emerged which renders the concept of racism an unfortunate – and bygone – historical transgression, a past that has been adequately redressed and is now best forgotten, even as informal, market-driven resegregation and exclusion proliferate in the private sector. This is a common sense further entrenched by the election and re-election of Barack Obama to the office of the US Presidency. If racial inequality persists today, so mainstream opinion goes, it is a function not of structural disadvantage in the form of dilapidated, dysfunctional schools; rampant and disproportional unemployment or underemployment; unequal access to loans and mortgages; unequal or no health care; police harassment, profiling, and mass incarceration of literally millions of people of color. It is a product, rather, of poor character. This commitment to colorblindness or racelessness, Goldberg asserts, is reinforced by – indeed an extension of – a neoliberal logic that translates all social problems into individual misfortune or misdeed. As a consequence, racist expression and exclusion are denied their social origin and systemic content, reduced to matters of private discrimination or predilection.

Not only are racist commitments privatized, Goldberg asserts, they are also radically depoliticized. As a complex set of historical and contemporary injustices, racism is analytically banished from the realm of the political. The role of the state, political economy, segregation, colonialism, capital, class exploitation, and imperialism are excised from public memory and from accounts of political conflict. Politics, in short, becomes "culturalized," to invoke Mahmood Mamdani's useful phrase (2004: 17). Political antagonisms are transformed into reified cultural and religious differences played out in the private sector, while simultaneously "disappearing" or "evaporating" the workings of power altogether. The simultaneous individualization and depoliticization of the discourses of race and racism are symptoms, moreover, of the state's supposedly waning power in the wake of globalization. The neoliberal attack on "big government," coupled with the state's withdrawal from formal and direct modes of racial governance, Goldberg observes, has generated extensive concentration on civil society, civility, tolerance, and their racially inscribed boundaries. The resurrection of the discourses of civility and tolerance bespeaks not only the neoliberal triumph of individualism over and against the state, but also its commitment to depoliticizing the sources of political problems, as it ideologically reconstitutes "difference" as a reified cultural essence rather than as an effect of structured subordination or inequality (Brown 2006: 46). As Wendy Brown observes, when emotional and personal vocabularies are substituted for political ones, when historically conditioned suffering and humiliation are reduced to "difference" or "offense," calls for "tolerance" or "respect for others" are substituted for political transformation in the interests of social justice. Political action devolves into sensitivity training, and the possibilities for political redress dissolve into self-help therapy (Brown 2006: 16).

Conceptually challenged if not altogether analytically void, tolerance talk and tepid celebrations of multicultural diversity circulating within and outside the academy do not go nearly far enough in codifying or challenging ongoing racist violence and exclusion. Racial panics, especially against anyone identified (even mistakenly) as Muslim, have been spurred by terrorist attacks in an ever-expanding list of global cities, from New York, Washington, and Boston to Madrid, London, and Nairobi, and by acts of state terrorism in Guantánamo, Palestine, Iraq, Afghanistan, and Yemen. Headscarf hysteria has gripped Paris, and the Golden Dawn political party is emblematic of the return of organized fascism as a viable political bloc in Greece and beyond. Armed vigilante groups "patriotically" patrol the US border with Mexico as individuals assigned to neighborhood watch groups guard against racial non-belonging in gated communities in Florida, executing at will, as the case of Trayvon Martin attests. Proliferating encampments of the stateless number among the fates that await millions of economic migrants and political refugees. And the aftermath of manmade natural catastrophes blight the US Gulf Coast and Haiti, devastating communities of the racial poor. It is against all of these events that Goldberg's nuanced, textured analysis of state commitments to racial homogeneity and to neoliberal economics must be understood as a significant event in the history of race theorizing.

David Theo Goldberg's most recent book, *The Threat of Race* (2009), brings us closer still to what he calls the "racial global," and to war, violence, and death suffered in the name of race. The project was initially titled *The Death of Race*, a provocation meant to draw attention to a deeply disturbing contemporary paradox in which academicians, intellectuals, and political pundits across the ideological spectrum call for the conceptual "death of race" while contemporaneously racially produced death – as a result of avoidable war, state violence, crippling poverty, famine, disease – grows exponentially. Against rightwing logics proclaiming the end of racism or insistent calls from some on the left to return to the primacy of class and political economy, *The Threat of Race* seeks to unsettle theoretical concepts and modes of analysis that have passed uncritically into the common sense of recent "cutting-edge" race theory.

Yet despite such precise interventions, one notes in Goldberg's newest writing a different narrative voice, a shift in scholarly tone and analytic vocabulary, a passion and focus born of urgency yet committed to remaining "coolly critical, cutting and incisive" (2009: viii). The radical experimentation in prose style departs from predictable academic penchants and scholarly norms in an effort to draw readers' attention to argument rather than erudition – a genuine act of persuasion in an academy often enraptured with insular and arcane performance.

The stark assessment Goldberg issues and disturbing terminology he fashions to communicate the global "threat" of postracial presumption reflect his judgment of the securitizing logics at work in the US and similar societies he calls "self-strangulating" – societies in pursuit of the illusion of security and safety through power-assisted forms of social homogeneity that require the disappearance, the eradication of enemies, foreign or domestic, inevitably racially indexed. Against the fantasy of postracial global triumphalism, he compels our witness, and our critical response: to racially driven suffocation and asphyxiation ("buried, alive," "self-strangulation"); industrialized, globalized mass violence ("ethnoracial purging," "mutilation," "genocide," "duress," "disposability") capable of destroying, depriving, "evaporating death" itself; to marginality, segregation, and separation (the "warehoused," imprisoned, encamped, the "permanently temporary" and "rogue"); and the horror of nonbeing ("racial erasure," "racial evaporation," the "depersonalization of the damned"). An underlying motivation in crafting such a bald and bracing new lexicon, one suspects, is to challenge scholars existentially untouched by contemporary global crises because insulated, politically and intellectually, in what Susan Buck-Morss uncomfortably calls "theory-world" (2003: 8).

To be sure, Goldberg's bold yet comprehensive analysis of contemporary geopolitical sites of race points to a number of disturbing questions: How is it that we have arrived at a present so marked by racial humiliation, terror, and death, as these troubling images and tropes insist? And how have we come to imagine it as our moment of triumph, the achievement of a thoroughly deracinated new world order conceived variously in rubrics of "racial democracy," "multiculturalism," "ethnic pluralism," and "colorblindness"? And what is our path back from the brink of societal self-destruction? James Baldwin felt the urgency of similar questions in his pitched battle against the long, terrifying history of legal segregation in 1961. Yet he concluded his address to the Liberation Committee with a sense of possibility:

> We in this country now – and it really is one minute to twelve – can really turn the tide because we have an advantage that Europe does not have, and we have an advantage that Africa does not have, if we could face it. Black and white people have lived together for generations, and now for centuries. Now, on whether or not we face these facts everything depends. (Baldwin 2010: 15)

Against the relentless forms of market-driven segregation, social securitization, and containerization that mark the contemporary moment in North America and internationally, Goldberg urges us to a similar possibility, to "heterogeneous dispositions" and "dispositions of openness" which "offer an antidote to the conceit of holding things constant, to the arrogance of control" (2009: 368). Such dispositions require the forsaking of "guarantees of outcome" predicated on stability and predictability and acknowledging the inevitable and shared fact of our mutuality and vulnerability. North Americans still hold the advantage of their shared history of heterogeneity, if they could face it.

Part of the answer to societies historically and newly polarized and implosive lies in our refusal to participate in the willful amnesia that marks contemporary racial politics and engage rigorously the dense and diverse histories of modern globalizations. Extending the arguments elaborated throughout his work, Goldberg argues in the following conversations that post-racial or nonracial presumption marks the culmination of the regionally and often temporally specific racist logics – naturalist, historicist, and their colorblinding extension – constitutive of liberal modernity, its drive to state sovereignty, its political economy, its architectural design and social spacing, its socio-intellectual authority, and its moral reason.

Goldberg consistently rejects scholarly efforts to consign racism to the ancient or premodern past, as well as the inclination to concede its modern expression but isolate its manifestation in the singularity of the Nazi state or the South African apartheid state. Race is foundational to becoming modern. Indeed, the historic sweep from the medieval to the modern is in fact "reflected in the shifts from religion as a dominant public frame for structuring and interpreting social life to the *civic religion of race* as prevailing fabric of public arrangement and imaginative hermeneutics" (Goldberg 2009: 2, emphasis added). By the eighteenth century, as much in Europe as in its colonies, race, Goldberg argues, assumed the status of a political theology – compelling popular belief through intellectual illumination or, when necessary, more direct forms of persuasion – mobilizing every resource available from scientific rationality and moral philosophy to the edifying force of a police baton or a soldier's bayonet. "The political theology of race," he maintains, "seeks to account for origins, circumscribes rationality, motivates the social fabric and its constitutive forms of exclusion, orders police and grounds power, liberating cruelty from constraint" (2009: 254).

Throughout his body of work, Goldberg boldly and bravely addresses the most combustible issues of the day – the conflict between Israel and Palestine, the US-led war in Iraq and Afghanistan and its "born again

racism" at home, the political theology of race in South
Africa and elsewhere – in academic and public contexts
where one is today all too often surveilled and harassed,
if not overtly censored, for such views. This is the threat
of race in a putatively raceless world. Such darkly challenging times well reflect what Goldberg has called "the
paradoxes of racism":

> Never again, and yet again and again, even now, never
> more so before our very eyes. Seeing but not; seeing but
> not believing; believing but believing immediately not my
> problem, our problem; seeing and believing but frozen
> from action, too distracted or busy or unconcerned to do
> anything about it; acting but not in concert, not concert-
> edly. (2009: 156)

Goldberg's eloquent commentary carries both insight
and warning, echoing with chilling appropriateness the
powerful conclusion of Hannah Arendt's *Origins of
Totalitarianism*: "Isolation may be the beginning of
terror; it certainly is its most fertile ground; it always is
its result. This isolation is, as it were, pretotalitarian; its
hallmark is impotence insofar as power always comes
from men acting together, 'acting in concert'... isolated
men are powerless by definition"(1951: 477). It is such
horrible potentialities, increasingly perceived as inevita-
bilities in a contemporary context saturated with violence, terror, and authoritarian tendency, that Goldberg
has passionately committed to both challenge and
dissolve.

Throughout his career, Goldberg has written and
spoken brilliantly and courageously about the history
of race, racism, politics, identity, power, the state, and
social justice. He has also been an ardent defender of

higher education, one of the few remaining, as a site where such critical inquiry can take place. This, at a time when the university and specifically the humanities have been subject to ongoing decades-long assault, first, as Christopher Newfield (2011) explains, in the form of the "culture wars" and then in the form of the "budget wars." As a public intellectual, Goldberg embodies in both thought and action the ideal and the practice of what it means to reclaim higher education in general, and the humanities more specifically, as sites of possibility that embrace the idea of a "fugitive" democracy, not merely as a mode of governance, but also as a means of dignifying heterogeneous populations of people so they can become fully free to claim their moral and political agency. This book accordingly is structured to bring together in clearly delineated and interactive ways both the relations and tensions around Goldberg's theorizing of race and its sitings across various contexts of political economy and culture. The first five chapters thus focus more directly on theoretical lines of analysis, and the latter five on an analysis of various contextual articulations.

Goldberg has argued in theoretically insightful and profound ways what it means to defend the university as a potential counter-public sphere, one that opens up and sustains public connections through which people's fragmented, uncertain, incomplete narratives of identity, history, and agency are valued, preserved, and made available for exchange, while being related, analytically, to wider contexts of politics and power. He has argued for a reinvigorated humanities alive to the challenge of regrounding liberal modernity's racially inscribed notions of ethics, justice, and morality across existing disciplinary terrains. And he has raised both a sense of urgency and a set of relevant questions about what kind of humanities would be suited to the twenty-first-century university and its global arrangements as part of a larger project of addressing the most pressing issues that we face globally. As Baldwin reminds us, the time remains one minute to midnight.

I

Race to modernity

Susan Searls Giroux: You grew up in apartheid South Africa, where you engaged, as you have put it, in "years of struggle against apartheid on picket lines and around parliament, through the mists of tear gas and protest slogans and closing down the college campus," then moving to the US to attend graduate school in New York City and finding there "Reagan's brand of 'new racism' reeled all about too. There it lay, not quite invisibly," you write, "in the conditions producing both homelessness and homeboys, dramatically differentiated employment rates across race and hypersegregation" [Goldberg 2002b: 422–3]. It is against this backdrop that you map the personal and political contexts that informed your transition from youthful activism to write on the "philosophical foundations of racism," which, radically revised, became the basis for *Racist Culture* [1993]. You produced, in short, a comprehensive philosophical archeology of racial conceptualization where none had existed before, as part of your efforts to "throw down a gauntlet to the discipline of philosophy, to challenge its parochialism, its self-possessed denial, its blindness to its own traumatic implication in the history of racist reproductions, its sweeping of its own stench behind that veil of ignorance" [Goldberg 2002b: 423]. Can you talk about why you chose to intervene in what you saw unfolding all around you in Cape Town and then New York in the form of a deeply historical and philosophical treatise on racism, especially as we seem to find ourselves at a time when there is a great deal of suspicion and cynicism about the significance of "academic" interventions in the worldly space of politics? Your own formation as an intellectual seems to suggest a need to rethink common-sense distinctions between theory and practice, the so called "ivory tower" and the space of "realpolitik."

David Theo Goldberg: Let me start with the autobiographical and thread back into the conceptual question. I grew up in a middle-to-increasingly-upper-middle class home, a fairly liberal South African family. Extended members of the family were engaged in politics from the center to the left, the older members being more centrist in nominally opposing apartheid under a liberally driven sense of what living in South Africa might be as a nonracial society and voted and acted accordingly; the younger members of the family engaged in antiracist activity of various kinds, mainly campus politics, which to some degree took on life-and-death circumstances. A cousin, closest to me growing up, identified himself as a mixed-race person living with and interacting with other mixed-race people in Cape Town, and continues to live out his life forty years later in a quite provocative way, refusing to give in to certain aspects of racial politics in South Africa, much to the chagrin of the rest of the family. So we have this not quite entire gamut, because the entire gamut would include proto-nationalists and the like, who were absent, sometimes refused. Another cousin wanted to marry the daughter of a notable apartheid government cabinet minister, and both families intervened to prevent it, liberalism and racial nationalism, Jewishness and Calvinism running headlong into each other. At the same time, as with almost every family like this in South Africa, there were members of the household – I hesitate for all the obvious political reasons to say quite full members – who as domestic labor lived with us and were very much part of an extended family, socially intimate. As I grew into teenage years, living social life on a beach, I would go off into townships with friends of my age and begin to engage with black people. Older men invited us into their homes in the townships, to engage in illicit transactions. I realize retrospectively that there was more than the illicit activity holding us together; there was a – I'll call it – humaneness, treading on the ground of humanism Paul Gilroy continues to push provocatively and productively, that drew us in, drew us together. There were common exchanges around politics, sports, discussions about sexuality. There were conversations about social life, about political issues of the day. It's those things that one realized flew very dramatically and very immediately in the face of apartheid. We were transgressing apartheid as we were doing this, but it also prompted very deep questions about the forms of race denial and human denial with which we were confronted on the most immediate basis.

Everything in South Africa then, and to some, though lesser, degree now, had a racial dimension to it, so that the forms of repression, which were so deep around race, could only inevitably pervade every other aspect of social-political life, in both trivial and nontrivial ways. From discipline at school to everyday policing in the street, the forms of invasiveness were at every level of existence, concerning not just the more obvious traditional senses of political activity. And as a thinking teenager I began to question those forms of repression and to realize that they marked and ordered every aspect of our everyday being.

I grew up in a house on a hill looking out to Robben Island across Table Bay. It was literally the first view of my morning, every morning of my teenage and into university life. And so I was faced daily by the question of racially founded privilege and the costs at which it was purchased. This wasn't just about Mandela, although he symbolized something to us even in the mid- to late 1960s and early 1970s. It was a matter of the symbolism of a future South Africa that would not be beholden to these pervasive forms of repression. That became evident every day I woke up. It was a formative part of waking experience. I can't say everybody had this experience, or faced this question explicitly. I just happened to live on a hill overlooking Robben Island But every time there was a piece of news about somebody dying on Robben Island or in other spaces of incarceration, about Steve Biko being beaten to death by the police in 1977 or forms of political repression like those in 1976 or earlier in the 1972 trade union strikes, and so on, these issues became more palpable, and one couldn't help but take a stand. Even if you refused to take an explicit stand on these things, it was a stand, right? So the more conscious one became, the more inevitably present to one these questions were.

For black people in the townships it was more immediate and more direct, especially post-1976: black urban space was being made ungovernable. The privilege for those of us at almost completely white universities itself came into question. Black and mixed-race students would only be admitted to designated white and privileged universities if they could show that their desired course of study was not available at designated black colleges. So black students would design seemingly anomalous curricula, like pre-medicine and archeology (perhaps interdisciplinarily they were way ahead of the curve!).

In the early 1970s in South Africa, debates in the social sciences and the humanities, in which I was training, were very largely around the class/race question in the wake of Althusser. There were heated debates around interpellation, around repressive and ideological state apparatuses. We were reading Fanon seriously, not so much *Black Skin White Masks* [1956], which became a text *du jour* of the northern hemisphere academy in the late 1970s and early 1980s. We took inspiration from what we read as revolutionary texts, *Wretched of the Earth* [1963], *A Dying Colonialism* [1965], and *Toward the African Revolution* [1969]. These texts spoke to us about the possibility of Zimbabwe and Mozambique being free societies (painful to think of the former in these terms today), of throwing off colonial repression. So when I left South Africa in 1977 and arrived in New York in 1978, it was that set of experiences I brought with me.

Going into a graduate program in philosophy that was consumed with the questions of philosophy of language, the philosophy of science, epistemology, very traditional philosophical questions, I began looking around for other inspirations. Edward Said had just published *Beginnings* [1978] and was about to publish *Orientalism* [1979]. I sat in a class of his on Gramsci, Althusser, and Foucault at Columbia. I was searching around in the corpus of philosophy, in that form of philosophy to which I was being subjected as a graduate student, in order to come to terms with a project that would speak to me, and that I could speak to from my own experience. That struggle over race and class had stayed with me, those South African debates. They were still very reductionistic; they were concerned with Althusser, to use Foucault's term, as the counterhistory within the Marxist corpus, which is why it was seized on within the context of South Africa in the 1970s. It offered a counter to the reductionism of a Harold Wolpe, to some extent Martin Legassick and Stanley Trapido or Ben Magubane, of racism as an epiphenomenal ideological formation, the force of which was always driven by class and the form of class would define the form of racial arrangement being expressed. This always struck me as a weak response regarding the force of race. Race seemed so obviously a much thicker, less epiphenomenal and dependent form of engagement, of social being and arrangement, of politics than class reductively was able to account for. Those seeking to reduce race to shadow effects of class struck me as necessarily paying no attention to the complexities of the racial.

SSG: It functions as an evasion, actually …

DTG: ... an evasion, yes. The material conditions were not unimportant, of course. They set the limits of possibility. But they certainly didn't define or comprehend the self-determinations around questions of race. When I was confronted with figuring out a dissertation project, there was very little, no philosophical dissertations about race. There was a bit of analytic philosophy around race and morality that addressed race, from the liberal point of view, as an irrelevant category. So I began a kind of archeology trying to trace the philosophical and intellectual considerations out of which this commitment to race as a morally irrelevant category emerged from the likes of Hobbes onwards. And this archeology became, predictably, much influenced by Foucault. It became a genealogy of modernity. So you can begin to see in what became *Racist Culture* the emergence and elaboration of forms of racially shaped liberalism as a centerpiece of philosophical modernity.

An anecdote bears out the force and pervasiveness, even the hegemony, of this philosophical disposition regarding race in the English-speaking academy of the time. Gerry Cohen, an analytic Marxist who in the early 1980s was writing very effectively about "world-ownership," about property, subjectivity, and power [see Cohen 1986], came to give a talk for my graduate program. At the reception he asked me, "So what are you working on?" And I said, "The philosophical foundations of racism." He clearly balked, was taken aback, and blurted out, not unsympathetically, "You mean racism *has* philosophical foundations?" And it was that, not just ignorance, but blindness, the veil of ignorance, you might say, to push the point, which I took as an

expression of a much broader, wider, deeper set of eva-
sions, as you called them ...

SSG: Right, a refusal to know.

DTG: An absolute refusal in which these questions were
not even on the map and an excavation of the philosophical history that produced them was just starting
up. This was pre-Skip Gates's *"Race," Writing and Difference* [Gates and Appiah 1992], pre-*Racial Formations* [Omi and Howard 1986], it was just at the time
that Stuart Hall was writing "Race, Articulation and
Societies Structured in Dominance" [1980], *Policing the
Crisis* [Hall et al. 1978] was not being widely read yet,
even though it had been written three to four years
earlier. Said's *Orientalism* was just taking hold of imaginations, of imaginative geographies, so it gives you a
sense of how deep the silences ran. There was an emerging tension between a view that race and racism couldn't
possibly have any philosophical or more broadly intellectual underpinnings and the counterhistory concerned
to uncover exactly the intellectual underpinnings race
and racism had been afforded throughout modernity. I
wasn't alone. I quickly found a group of young African-
American philosophers who became very influential in
my socialization into a set of philosophical debates.
With them a society formed, founded by Al Prettyman
in his living room on Broadway, into which circle I was
welcomed, the New York Society for Black Philosophy,
which included Cornel West, Howard McGary, Tommy
Lott, Bill Lawson, Lucius Outlaw; it was through the
Society I met Angela Davis. It became very instrumental
in opening up the American Philosophy Association to

engaging these questions. If you attend an APA meeting today you will see all kinds of panels addressing issues of race that would not have been possible without this moment in the early 1980s.

SSG: One of the primary theoretical concerns in *The Racial State* [Goldberg 2002a] has been to differentiate historically between the shifting logics and practices – moral and legal, economic and political – within specific racially configured states. Principally you discuss the movement from what you call "racial naturalism" to "racial historicism," and the corollary transition in forms of racial rule from brute force to the rule of law. You describe the current moment in terms of a new regime of racially conceived truth – what you call states of racelessness.

Your most recent work, however, seems to indicate a return to brute force and violence in the interests of racial rule. I'm thinking in particular of your discussion of *racial americanization*, the militarization of its domestic and foreign policy, but also your analysis of the state of Israel and the simultaneous elaboration of what you call *racial palestinianization*. As in the discussion of the US, you unveil a kind of Hobbesian scene around racial palestinianization concerning war becoming permanent, relationships of force, the suspension of rights, and so on. Your comments raise so many questions, but I'll focus on two primarily.

First, how is it that what you've called "naturalistic" logics and the use of violence seem to re-emerge and come to the fore in the context, particularly in the US, though I suspect at least nominal support globally, of a commitment to racelessness or race-transcendence?

And, second, does this bespeak another order of brute force altogether – what you call, after Achille Mbembe [2003], "necropolitics"?

DTG: Racial naturalism is the name I give to the set of claims that those considered not European or white, or not of European or to some significant degree white descent, are inherently inferior – naturally so – to those who are. Racial historicism, by contrast, is the set of claims that those not European or white, or not of European descent, are historically immature by comparison, and that the more mature have an obligation to school the less mature until they are capable of making good judgments for themselves, can thus rule themselves well (the civilizing mission). As I indicate in *The Racial State*, these two views don't preclude each other; they become more or less dominant in relation to historical circumstances. You can find both views held by the same person to different ends and purposes, or at different times; or held in the same state at different moments. They come and go; while one might be dominant, even to a degree hegemonic, that does not preclude the taking up of the logic of the other to certain purposes and under certain conditions. Sepulveda in mid-sixteenth-century Spain represents naturalism; Las Casas represents racial historicism in his resistance to enslaving the Indios of the Americas. But Las Casas himself owned African slaves, blind to the contradiction precisely by his racial naturalism with respect to Africans. Naturalism dominates European racial consciousness from the fifteenth well into the nineteenth century, underpinning modern slavery; historicism serves as naturalism's resistance, the understanding of the racial in the name of which abolition is largely driven, and becomes dominant in the wake of emancipation. World War II, arguably, is the ultimate contestation between these warring racial conceptions.

Now 9/11 seems to have opened up a space in which naturalism gets re-invoked. Muslims have been re-naturalized, so to speak. The language in the 2012 US presidential campaign about a large percentage of the population being "moochers and takers" (47 percent in Romney's account, 30 percent in Paul Ryan's) naturalizes a set of cultural claims, reinserting among conservatives naturalist commitment insinuatingly into their traditional "poverty of culture" concerns. In invading Iraq, you can see historicist assertions at work: the US will help to acculturate Iraqis into acquiring democratic values and institutional structures and practices. It is not that they are inherently incapable of them; quite the contrary. They have just not had the opportunity historically to nurture them, which America will now educate them into doing, cultivate in them, in short, civilize them. Here (and in Afghanistan too), one finds in the dominant American position the interlacing of a historicist with a naturalist conception: alongside the insistence on acculturating democratic disposition can be found the insistence of murderous tendencies, the resort to violence seen as "their natural way" of settling differences. Among many Israelis you find a similar bifurcation regarding Palestinians. This trajectory of racial conception arcs from the Inquisition at modern Europe's founding to Europe's latter-day self-fortressing to hold at bay perceived pollutants of "real" Euro-identity.

SSG: And you've also said that racelessness insistent on historical amnesia leaves no other analytical alternative to this kind of biologized naturalism.

DTG: Underlying these differentiated claims is a deeper, longstanding concern, namely, the management of heterogeneities in any society. Such management assumes two dominant forms: first, acknowledging mixture and "diversity" but insisting that all social subjects be bound by the prevailing social and cultural values of those dominant in the society (I call this the insistence on "Euro-mimesis"); and, second, the recourse to violence where management through mixture fails, where subjugated subjects more or less self-consciously refuse Euro-mimetic imposition. Violence is usually rationalized in terms of naturalizing forms of representation. So the notion of a permanent war opens up a space for imposing violent technologies of management directly, viscerally, on people. The longer the violence lingers and is met with resistant counter-violence, the likelier it is that historicizing rationalizations will dissipate, even disappear, and the boldness of the violence will ramp up. One can probably trace this waxing and waning in specific cases, like Iraq or the Palestinian Territories, in the war on terror, in the pacification program, more recently in US media characterization of Egyptians "not having democracy in their political DNA," and in the rationalization of "black on black" murders driving the reversal of George Zimmerman as victim and Trayvon Martin as aggressor, as perpetrator. The more pacified, the more likely one will find historicizing logic: Look, they are turning into democrats just like us, let's support them. And when pacification is not going so well, the state of naturalizing logic returns ...

SSG: ... they only understand violence ...

DTG: ... uh huh. Let's drop a few more bombs on them, shock and awe, drones at a distance, collateral damage is just the price to be paid. You mentioned "racelessness." Racelessness is the sort of tabula rasa of race, the wiping clean of the dirt of racist history. It fashions an empty space that can then be filled by the possibility of one form of rationalization or another according to the dictates of the day. It sublimates the force of violence beneath a regime of truth insistent that racially skewing institutional structures and racist violence are both long past. It tethers the make-believe – the compulsions – of violence to the fantasy of a world rid of racial privilege. Make-believe is both a making up and a forcing, a compelling into a given frame of reference. Anchoring truth in anything outside of itself, outside its terms and frames of reference, is made mute. It is auto-generative ...

SSG: ... no need for legitimization ...

DTG: ... and in that sense also auto-immune. In being auto-immune, it represses – buries, alive – its own contradictions, its potential implosiveness.

SSG: One of the most striking achievements of *Racist Culture* (and a theme upon which you further elaborate in *The Racial State*) is its substantive analysis of philosophical liberalism's investment in the discourses of race and racism, locating its conceptual appeals in Hobbes, Locke, Rousseau, Kant, Bentham, and Mill, to name but a few. The paradox of liberal modernity, you argue, is this:

> As modernity commits itself progressively to idealized principles of liberty, equality, and fraternity, as it increasingly insists upon the moral irrelevance of race, there is a multiplication of racial identities and the sets of exclusions they prompt and rationalize, enable and sustain. Race is irrelevant, but all is race. The more abstract modernity's universal identity, the more it has to be insisted upon, the more it needs to be *imposed*. [Goldberg 1993: 6]

It is an irony that extends from the Enlightenment to contemporary calls for colorblindness, a commitment that was supposed to usher in a postracist era. Why has this so emphatically not been the case?

DTG: The commitment to colorblindness in the US emerges post-abolition, indeed post-Reconstruction. You see the first explicit expression of it in Justice Harlan's minority dissent in *Plessy v. Ferguson* in 1896, where he explicitly invokes the notion of colorblindness. He is dismayed by the majority's insistence on segregation to maintain white supremacy and dominance in America. He argues that whites will have nothing to fear if the playing field is leveled in the sense of making it possible for all people to compete because whites already have such a leg up and would continue to dominate competitively because of accumulated wealth, education, networks of power, and the like.

It's interesting that from *Plessy* through the end of World War II, the notion of colorblindness was not in wide circulation. There is one popular book by Margaret Halsey just after World War II titled *Color Blind* [1946]. She was writing about race right after the war, the exclusion of black soldiers from dance halls and public accommodations, calling for a social commitment to being colorblind as a response. The war boosts the policy commitment to colorblindness in the name of liberalism's formal equality. Colorblindness, and racelessness more generally, receives another boost from the neoliberal embrace of Ronald Reagan and Margaret Thatcher in the 1980s.

So, one has to trace the arc around the recourse to colorblindness from *Plessy* to the attempt at legislating the Racial Privacy Act in California in 2004 and recent Supreme Court restrictions on affirmative action and racial determinations of the Voting Rights Act. The language of the Racial Privacy Act, promoted in the name of the "Civil Rights Initiative," may have failed at the ballot box but nevertheless reveals perfectly the neoliberal logic of race and the racial logic of neoliberalism. It's not the "death of race act," so to speak, or the "racial erasure act," or the "eradicating racism act." It is the "privatization of race act." In striking neoliberal terms, it's the undertaking to protect the private expression of *racism* from government intervention, even as the state is purging from itself any use of *race* for legislative or policy consideration.

Racelessness, then, of which colorblindness in the US is one articulation, is expressed variously in Europe, in post-apartheid South Africa, in Latin America. Racelessness is deeply embedded in the project of neoliberalism and, in short, in privatization. It is really the protection, the privatization, of discrimination, of segregation, of hypersegregation. You see it most palpably in the Katrina moment, which brought it to light, allowed us to catch a glimpse of it, if only fleetingly, for it would be covered over quickly. Or in the Trayvon Martin case, where Zimmerman was out to protect private property by profiling the teenager. Racelessness is the privatization of racism protected from government restriction, so that racism becomes untouchable by the state.

This is tied up with another deep question, having to do with social approaches to demographic and cultural heterogeneity and homogeneity, the comforts people take and think they feel "naturally." People have come to think they feel naturally at ease in "being around their own kind," in living with those of their own culture, in choosing, they think freely and of their own volition, naturally to exclude those they categorize as not belonging to whatever patria that they've been given over to being part of. This, too, is the naturalization of the social.

SSG: I have two related questions in mind concerning homogeneity. The body of your work reflects an abiding interest in the co-constitutive relationship between modernity and race as well as a challenge to conceptualizations of race and racism as pre- or anti-modern and archaic. It reflects, too, an indebtedness to Zygmunt Bauman [1989], whose account of modernity similarly stresses order and ordering systems, as opposed to the more typical emphases on industrialism, capitalism, secularism, or democracy. Though the logic of ordering is clearly implicit in these other modern endeavors, I'm curious about why this particular focus for you?

Relatedly, you suggest, again following Bauman, that modernity's insistence on order necessarily entails a pre-occupation with disorder, and an attendant ambivalence toward those groups perceived to be disruptive or destructive of ordering ambition and design. In European modernity, for him, the archetypical outsiders, the group least "like us," were Jews. Heterogeneity is marked as a problem or a pathology. In your work, "homogeneity" has become, by your own description, a kind of *idée fixe*; it is a driving force in the construction of a cohesive social identity and moral community, in modern state formation, in the racially ordered postmodern city. Can you further explain why the artifice of homogeneity, in denial or repressed, continues to hold such significance?

DTG: Well, the focus on order, of course, follows from my abiding concern with the ways modernity is marked increasingly from at least the eighteenth century with classification schemes in disciplines like biology and natural philosophy. This concern with classification also characterizes the contemporaneous emergence of state bureaucracies so central to modern governance. The onset of insurance, actuarial tables, formal record keeping, census taking: all these social technologies become formalized in the latter half of the eighteenth century. Census taking becomes a key in colonial control around this time, for example, by the British in India, as Bernard Cohn [1987] so importantly revealed, and was mandated by the revolutionary United States in its founding Constitution. So this focus on classification and order – the two obviously go together – comes to define modern governmentality.

Classification schemes immediately take on a racial dimension, in both natural philosophy and governmentally. And it's that relationship, articulating the project of Man with that of ordered governance, that is sewn together through various forms of racial project. As a rationality of governing and self-governance, liberalism comes into its own with the Enlightenment, as a philosophy of the individual and of the modern state, and their co-defining relation. John Locke, really a pre-liberal philosopher, is key here in the late seventeenth century. He brings into relational focus self-understanding, political governance, and colonial order (Locke was instrumental in writing the Constitution of the colonial Carolinas, which ceded to citizens "absolute power over their Negro slaves"). So there is a compelling triangulation at liberalism's founding between life's governance as an individualizing project and liberalism as a governing project, both racially articulated. The autonomy of the individual and the sovereignty of populations are circumscribed for and by those taken to have rationality. And rationality both has long underpinned and been circumscribed by a racial dimension. Modernity is defined by this set of conceptions. It was thinking these things together that brought me to the question of homogeneity and heterogeneity.

An abiding presumption of social theory is that it's natural to want to be with, to seek out, one's own; that somehow this is a natural condition of human existence. In its universalizing commitment to equality, even liberalism has taken this assumption at face value, as a limiting condition on turning principle into policy. A conserving social sameness is taken up as a mark of the human. If a racial conception for modernity is the secularization of the religious, it inherits from religious self-understanding – and naturalizes – this seeking out of "one's own," the fabrication of origins, of common heritage, the extension of kinship. Taking leave from such naturalized commonality thus constitutes a rupture, a radical excision, something that undoes stability and order. So homogeneity becomes the abiding assumption here. When you question homogeneity, you seem either irrational, unduly provocative, or revolutionary, where revolutionary is not necessarily a good thing. And one who questions in this way risks being cast asunder, excommunicated racially as religiously, in order to save, to preserve, homogeneity. You can quickly see how racial expression, racial formation, racial articulation, racial arrangement, become "natural," really a naturalizing expression of this presumption.

This set of presumptive commitments struck me as palpably wrong. Human beings have always moved. People in villages 20 kilometers apart somehow seek to find out what's going on in the other village. When kids are told not to go over there, curiosity gets the better and more often than not they wander over to see what's so prohibitive. Brought up on "Don't marry into that family," youth will find a way of falling in love with the out of reach. It doesn't always work this way, but curiosity about those things unknown to us is in part what has driven human beings, the epistemological drive. Curiosity, we are told, kills the cat. And so thinking about the question of heterogeneity involves thinking about translation in the broad cultural in addition to the narrowly linguistic sense. It involves undoing, trying to de-anchor the naturalizing presumption of belonging, which is after all a confluence of "being" and romantic "longing." This involves not just focusing on being, that condition of stasis, of being with; it has to do also with a romantic imaginary that exceeds the givenness, the fixities, of "being." This then drives the curious to the unknown, to engage with those one's not expected to.

To better understand heterogeneities requires thinking about the impositions of homogeneity. Homogeneity is a repression, a restriction. It can only sustain itself through delimitation, through strictures that are imposed, through ordinances, rules, and regulations that require one to do this and not that, to regularize life, to preserve privilege and reserve the right to belonging. The current fight to delimit voting rights in the US, for instance, is the baldest effort to *pre-serve* homogeneity, to sustain its force in the face of a demographic logic destined to bring about its demise. It's the only way it can sustain itself. And in that sense it is deeply "unnatural," imposed by those capable of asserting the power to do so. Heterogeneities excite, conjure possibility, challenge the established, push people to think anew, to break with regularity, to open up possibilities, to extend horizons, even to the point of failure. For from failure, too, important lessons about the possible are to be learned.

This social structuring around homogenization as containment and curtailing in contrast to a sociality predicated on heterogeneities reveals two less obvious ways of understanding racial attribution, racisms, and their logics of operation.

First, "whiteness" and "blackness" are not simply racial identifications. They represent class positions: the former of relative privilege, the latter of disprivilege. Whiteness and blackness are tied to people who represent a range of phenotypical characteristics. But more complexly they also represent differentiated class positions that people of different phenotypes can inhabit, can assume or be ascribed. One can be phenotypically or culturally black and enter that class position of whiteness, acquiring privilege, even if limited in relation to phenotypically white people in that privileged position, that class position called whiteness. This reveals the velocity with which one may fall in and out of the condition of whiteness.

There is a second issue, this one regarding the very meaning of "racism." Ruth Wilson Gilmore [2007: 28] compellingly has characterized racism as the foreshortening of life and life's possibilities. The humiliations, degradations, indignities, and modes of exclusion constituting racisms directly or indirectly foreshorten life. Racially produced exclusions restrict the resources and possibilities in the absence of which life would be extended, would not be foreshortened were it not for those forms of racism. So racism is constitutively related to a necropolitics. This relation of restriction, exclusion, and the foreshortening of life and life's possibilities to necropolitics, to the politics of racially produced death, is the indelible mark of modernity's arc, from the mid-fifteenth century to the death of Trayvon Martin among so many others today. It is the arc of race, of the racial, to the modern, to modernity.

2

Global racialities

SSG: In an early manuscript version you described *The Threat of Race* in general terms as concerned with "the legacies of death and violence in the name of race," an attempt to unravel the paradox of mounting racially prompted death and its threats that seems to have accompanied conceptual calls of late for "the death of race." You describe the project as "trying exactly to fashion a different kind of analytic vocabulary, and wide global trajectory fashioned in terms of regional configurations – racial americanization, palestinianization, europeanization, latinamericanization, southern-africanization, and their contemporary implications for thinking about raceless racisms in the present/future." You tie this conceptualization explicitly to rejecting the concept of racialization. Can you elaborate on these concerns?

DTG: This growing concern emerged out of writing *The Racial State* early in the millennium. The notion of "racialization" is used far too readily and easily, covering over numerous related concerns. First, more often than not one cannot tell from the context in which "racialization" is used whether it is being invoked descriptively or normatively. Are we just describing racial conditions, arrangements, relationships, and interactions? Which of these is one characterizing, and is it simply a description of those conditions or is there a normative project at work? It cannot simply be assumed that every time "racialization" is used the user means to reject or find degrading that to which the use purports to refer. (Is it the broad social fabric, institutional orders, legal arrangements, policies, etc.?) There is some ambiguity about whether one is simply characterizing a set of racial conditions or racial meanings, to use Winant's [1994] conception, or racial attributions, and so on, or whether one is ascribing racisms to whatever racialization is purporting to refer. And if racisms, what are the forms that these racisms take? How do they differ from one instance to another, from the US to Britain, France, or the Netherlands to Germany, Latin America to South Africa? Or even from one attribution of the term to another?

SSG: Yes, students are tripping over that all the time …

DTG: It's interesting: as the presumption of racelessness takes hold of conventional political imaginaries with the turn of the millennium, "racialization" colonizes the analytic imaginations of critical scholars. In a sense they mirror each other. Those accepting that there is – or can be – "racism without race" cannot also assume that racial conception and racism are identical, or inevitably connected. I think "racialization" really is a sloppy notion. Both students and faculty, our colleagues, repeatedly invoke the notion, and we're supposed to say … ah yes, we know precisely what you're talking about, when actually we often don't. Sometimes we may be able to tell from the context what is meant, but this is the exception proving the rule. So that's the first thing. The second is that racialization is tied mostly – almost in the same breath – to a critical analytic that will usually claim race to be an empty category. But if it's an empty category, it does no work at all. It's empty. It gets filled by something else. I've made that claim myself about the emptiness of race …

SSG: Well, you say it's at one and the same time analytically empty and too full, too freighted with multiple meanings, too amenable to being stretched across any number of discursive orders …

DTG: Right. But race is filled by something that's not itself, so to speak, by sets of social conditions, by articulations with class and gender and other ethnic and cultural forms of expression, and the like. Race becomes the placeholder for these conditions and expressions. And so I want to make something else than race do the analytic work. I call this "racial regionalizations." I want a concept that would enable a generalization, a generalizability. I lit on "regionalization," on a conceptual configuration that is a region, because I wanted to make an argument about different geographies having different, if intersecting, histories of racial expression and racist exclusion, of racial threats and forms of death and delimitation of life, in a sense of different racially driven political "personalities." "Regionalization" – at

---

once made and constantly having to be reproduced through reinforcement – sites the kind of work for filling in the historical background and its modes of articulation, its expressions in contemporary terms.

I've chosen to focus contingently on some regions because they've been particularly pernicious, expressive, and dominant in the historical formation around racial questions: the United States – "americanization" as a form of expression; and "palestinianization," because it is so present with us and yet its racial expression has been so denied. Likewise with Europe for related, though different, reasons, most notably, in the wake of World War II. You can't mention the word "race" regarding human beings in mainland Western Europe (Britain, as so often, is the exception here). If you do, you'll be looked at like you're either mad or awful, the kind of person everyone wants to avoid. It's very difficult to talk about race, even critically, in relation to human beings in Europe. By contrast, Latin America – latinamericanization – has a very different mode of racial expression and a different history producing it. And Southern Africa, in particular South Africa, although resonating more widely in the region, offers a different model, one that has been influential, politically and analytically, not only in the formulation of racial conditions but also in societies seeking to take leave, to distance themselves from racism. Think, relatedly, of the charge of "apartheid" leveled at a society not South Africa and of taking distance from South Africa to deny any locally lingering racial legacy.

Racial expression and racist delimitation differ in each of those regional arrangements. And contemporary recourse to racelessness takes on different expression in each region too, even as there are elements of convergence, interacting, intersecting, and reinforcing expressions inter-regionally. I wanted to provide a map of those variations and generalizations and their delimitation, their possibilities, as well as their traces. I was seeking a different analytics, one mindful that racial and racist expression in one region is not necessarily restricted to that region. These are the cartographics of race and racisms.

For example, there's been the insistence, post-9/11, on securing society. One could call this homeland security through social condomization, a prophylaxis. Social prophylaxis works by trying either to filter all social interaction through the sterilizing latex of securitizing technologies or to cut the society off from all social relation. The upshot of both is extensive paranoid (self-)surveillance: America increasingly in the first instance, North Korea founded on its basis in the second.

SSG: You address that specifically: "National (now reconceptualized as 'homeland') security has become the abiding insomnia of American paranoia. The logic of segregation, of isolation, accordingly has come to dominate United States foreign policy too" [2009: 98]. The upshot is a circumstance that radically undermines the obsessive drive to national security, as you conclude: "Racial Americanization externalized is the fuel – and fear – of terrorism internalized" [2009: 99]. Can you further elaborate on this relationship?

DTG: I have long made a similar point about apartheid South Africa: as it closed itself down, cutting itself and being cut off, it imploded. It made itself not immune from but more challenged by the very conditions it claimed to be restricting. So it's not simply a contradictory project, it's an inherently implosive one. Apartheid was not possible without support from outside South Africa. These globally distributed relations of support and challenge were not a sufficient but a necessary condition for both sustaining and dismantling apartheid. How are these relations of support and movements to challenge connected across regions, how do they fuel, influence, and impact as well as sustain each other? How was apartheid shored up, for example, by investments taking place elsewhere, but also how was it resisted through global coalitions, sometimes by the very same powers involved in the investments? Obviously, action on the ground was another necessary condition for both sustaining and challenging. Global support and local action came together in the 1980s and into the 1990s to intensify the processes in play.

Racial regionalization suggests a conceptual frame in terms of which to map the complex of racial arrangements and racist expression, and the grounds for elaborating a critical vocabulary and analytics for thinking about race in its interactive global reach. Scientific and social ideas circulate as people travel, emerging in specific contexts and then migrating as modernity becomes increasingly mobile. Robert Knox's views about racial anatomy were fashioned in early-ish nineteenth-century Southern Africa but infamously elaborated, proliferated, and exported once again upon his return to Britain at mid-century. Du Bois's antiracist analytics, fashioned in late nineteenth-century America and Berlin during his doctoral studies there, were refined in Philadelphia,

Atlanta, but also by his travels for the Pan-African Congresses in Europe as well as his later exile to Ghana. Similarly, Eric Voegelin saw his antiracist analysis, born in central Europe, transformed upon exile to the American South before World War II. Magnus Hirschfeld, who first coined the term "racism" in 1933, paid deep attention to the debates around race in Europe and the US as he traveled for the work for which he is best known on the science of sexuality, homosexuality, and "transvestitism" (another term he coined). The critical tradition regarding race that they and others helped to spawn, from Fanon and Arendt to Angela Davis, Stuart Hall, and others, equally materialized through such global circulation.

Now this global reach of race and the remaking of the global through, by, and in the name of race maps the contours of social homogenization and the segregated bounding of heterogeneous socialities.

SSG: Regarding the logics of homogenization and securitization, in *The Threat of Race* there is a tension between your notion of social "self-strangulation" (in the context of Israel and the US, which you so rigorously ground in histories of those racial states) and Derrida's notion of "auto-immunity disorder" in *Philosophy in a Time of Terror*, the diagnostic through which he engages terrorism and the war on terror. Derrida describes its self-destructive potential in the following terms: "[W]hat is put at risk by this *terrifying* autoimmunitary logic is nothing less than the existence of the world" [2003: 98]. This threat was initially produced by the United States during the Cold War and after, a kind of "suicide of those who welcomed, armed,

and trained [the terrorists]" [2003: 95]. The concepts
seem to capture different logics of a suicidal trajectory.
The question is, how different and in what way?

DTG: There are certainly parallels with Derrida's comments here. There is something quite compelling to both
the question of auto-immunity and its implosion: in the
attempt to produce an immunity by society for itself in
the face of proliferating heterogeneities and in setting
up the conditions that would produce this immunity, it
creates at once the conditions imploding it. As Derrida
puts it, this is a self-suicide. Suicide, of course, is always
at least of the self, a suicidal state or condition in which
producing that security to effect immunity also produces the means by which that immunity is undone,
undercut, or at least threatened. The technology used in
terrorism is often that used in state repression and coun-
ter-terrorist interventions, thus taking aim at the heart
of the technological apparatus itself. The fear thus produced, as Derrida expresses it, is always the fear of the
future. One projects into a future that is forever fearful
and that fear then undercuts the very conditions of
freedom that are supposedly being protected. Derrida is
right, of course. Hacking operates by taking on the very
logic of auto-immunity and virality, using their tools
against them. Hence the vigor with which it is being
prosecuted.

Obviously, the logics of self-strangulation about
which I talk here are connected. But it is a self-strangulation that is produced through externalization. Fight to
externalize danger to the outside, as Derrida would put
it, through auto-immunity, so that the dangers are dis-
tanced, placed outside. But that does two things: It

produces an outside that is dangerous, where the dangers are less controllable, that could go viral, from which there is no immunity, which reveals our very vulnerability. The outside looms larger and larger, constricting and constraining what one can do, where one can go, mindful even of the dangers "at home." At some point, in order to keep it as an outside, one has to be in it, to invade it, to make it to some degree one's own. The Israelis can say that they want to cede the Territories to the Palestinians as an independent state, but they keep on settling there, engaging in a process of "reclamation" of land they claim is not theirs but insist through repeated action that it is. The US incursions into Pakistan or Yemen exemplify another version of this general logic. In all these cases, longstanding implicit racial assumptions about the target populations mobilize the violations and violence at work.

Powerful societies assume and sustain their power, locally and globally, through extensions beyond themselves. They reach beyond the contained and constraining conditions of their own national borders, even as they might work to shore up the boundaries. It's not that borders are irrelevant. Any attempt in the face of contemporary conditions to cement national borders and boundaries as physical marks of the outside and the inside, however, ultimately flies in the face of other forces, especially economic ones, that tend to transgress fixations around material boundaries, even as they might invest to profit in them. There is a tendency that as national borderlines become more difficult to cement in place, local boundaries become more important. The more there is an undertaking to reify the national boundary, the more it's doomed to failure. Israel is among the most extreme exemplifications here, attempting to reify boundaries in terms of a cement wall (the US border with Mexico is another, South Africa's fenced borderline with Zimbabwe yet another). It's interesting how the "apartheid wall" has produced among Palestinians, especially youth even as young as 8 or 9 years old, a counter-commitment.

Put up a wall and the imaginary quickly follows that the wall is there to be traversed, to be taken down. How do you take it down? Well, for one, bits and pieces of the wall can be chipped away, so it starts to crumble at the edges or foundations. Knock out pieces, throw stones or rocks. All this is part of a broader culture of resistance, to the wall and what it stands for, in all sorts of creative ways and plays: walking through, floating over, cutting out parts of the wall. (I think here of the series of great Banksy images stenciled onto the "apartheid wall.") Unless every inch of the wall is policed round the clock – which then defeats the purpose of the wall itself – it's vulnerable in its very construction. All security walls, without failure, require supplementation: more wall, watchtowers, surveillance technology, militarized patrols, drones, sensors, and so on. Walls at once are both threatening and threatened.

So it's not just a factor of the implosion inside, internal to the walls, which is largely the logic of Derrida's argument, the contradictory implosiveness of the conditions of the walls' own structure. That's clearly at work. But there is a play, too, between the inside and the outside, and the implosion is exacerbated by the possibility of the outside invading the inside, undermining the division between the inside and the outside, not least with regard to the global configurations of the racial.

You can't always tell who belongs inside and who outside. That's a difficult thing to do, particularly among a heterogeneous population. Recall that repeated insistence of nativists to different-looking co-nationals to "go back to where you came from." As one clever response has put it: "So will you give me the cab fare to my neighborhood a couple of blocks away?" Even in a population forcefully rendered homogeneous, mimicking the homogeneous is always a possibility, as terrorist interventions now all too readily recognize.

What are the ways the inside extends itself outside without calling itself that? Self-containment always depends on the possibility of its extension in time, into the future. The very term "extension" suggests this. This extension is always dependent on the outside of itself, so the extension in time becomes also a spatial extension: for supplies, for cheap labor, for renewal. Eventually, even if self-containment is a real possibility, reproduction will exhaust its self-contained resources. Either one produces a population too large to sustain or the fact that the resources available are no longer sufficient to sustain social conditions requires externalities. The consequent proliferation of heterogeneities undercuts, quite radically, the very homogeneity the extension was seeking in the first place to sustain. So in the ecological imperative to go outside, trading, bartering, social intercourse is necessitated, as, too, is cultural renewal, the need for new ideas. Ultimately, for a new generation the attraction of the outside becomes compelling: we prefer what is over there, the exotic, the novel, different ways of being and doing. Curiosity drives us too: we want to know how others do things differently, "we" need "their" labor, "their" ideas, "their" energy for self-renewal in addition to whatever material resources their territories represent.

The inside always extends itself beyond itself and in doing so makes the self-containment vulnerable to its own demise. So as much as it is a function of auto-immunity, imploding upon itself from within, there are also the pressures from its extension into the outside. This, too, constitutes a logic of raciality …

SSG: … a kind of obesity …

DTG: … yes, a ballooning, bound to burst. Getting so large it has to smear itself across the universe, at which point its insides become totally vulnerable, devolve into its externalities. …

SSG: … or it's diabetic and parts of it just die …

DTG: … and get chopped off. These organic meta-phors reveal the racial logic attendant to the imaginaries of inside/outside. These racial logics of inside and belonging, contrasted with outside and lack, structure existing heterogeneities within the state, delimiting them and any emergent diversities, while also fueling the tensions across borderlines.

SSG: There is implicit in your comments about the global circuits of what you and Philomena Essed have called "race critical theory" [Essed and Goldberg 2002], in contrast to "critical race theory," a methodological observation regarding how to think about race and racism. Can you tease this out?

DTG: That's an astute recognition. Much of analysis about race globally indexed, critical and otherwise, has been comparativist. Comparativism presupposes the fixities of national boundaries, and a taken-for-granted premise that racial configurations are overwhelmingly bounded by the borders of nation-states. So the well-established tradition of ethnic and racial comparison – Carl Degler, Pierre van den Berghe, Jack Cell, Anthony Marx, etc. – historically has looked to similarities and contrasts between the US, Brazil, and South Africa. The tradition of critical race theory that emerges out of legal studies is methodologically bound in this way too, perhaps more understandably because law is so boundaried by the state it helps to set in place.

Comparativism starts from questionable premises – indeed, premises that require self-elevation of the observer to Sovereign judge, god-like if not God in fact. Social ideas, like the air we breathe, don't stop at the immigration desk. And racist formulations, like pollution, at once made and consumed by us, impact others too as their dirt harms us also. Ideas travel, circulate, return transformed to impact locals anew. Comparativism fails to recognize these transformative mobilities and impactful circulations. A different, more modest methodological disposition is necessitated to attend to the racial dimensions of globalities and the global dimensions of the racial. Comparativism, like the synchronic, may enable a deep dive into the specificities of locally bound racist expression and racial formulation; but to get at the overdeterminations that inevitably enable and impact racial configurations in all their complexities, their sources and elaborations, attending to relational considerations is imperative.

47

3

Modernity's civic religion

SSG: Both you and Derrida invoke a question of political theology. Derrida views the clash of Muslim fundamentalism and the US as one between two political theologies. How does this differ from your own analysis of a political theology of race?

DTG: Others have also used the notion of competing or conflicting political theologies, as competing fundamentalisms for power either regionally or more globally. The clash of civilizations has increasingly become the clash of political theologies. That's a fairly common, perhaps obvious, way of putting it. The theological aspects concern the anchoring of different sets of religious beliefs, different traditions, exacerbating the extremes of those conditions, but also a logic of presumed transcendentalism. The latter is less obvious. On the one side, evangelical Christian fundamentalism and, on the other, an extreme reading of Qur'anic fabrication, the extreme made to stand for the whole. Extremely reductive literalisms – which paradoxically embed their own versions of radical interpretation – mark both. One could characterize literalist fundamentalisms as interpretations not subject to interpretation, refusing them as they insist on their own most literalist one. The very condition of reading is destroyed. This is a not uncommon critique now among critical theorists.

The political theology of race came to me from an extended conversation with my close friend Achille Mbembe while thinking about political theology more generally. We had been teaching a graduate course together. What struck me was the ways in which race became, to use Eric Voegelin's characterization in 1933, a civic religion. Modernity's progressive self-secularization opened other forms of theological commitment and expression. Race is key among them, a secularization of the theological. Race increasingly configured that which the theological had served to do in political and sociological terms under earlier regimes of conception, order, and arrangement, but adding and elaborating over time specific forms of what Foucault later would call biopower. So race was conceived to operate in much the way that theology does: as belief commitments or convictions, as a regime of truth, as defining what could and could not be thought, said, and done, how and what to believe, what bodies count, what behavior to promote or restrict, who belongs to the community and who not. Like religion, race embeds claims of both origin and kinship. In short, what is at issue are beliefs, bodies, and behavior, culture and character.

So how to think about how race operates as a political theology, both generally and then in particular societies? South Africa offered a way of exemplifying this concretely, from which one could generalize to how political theology plays out differently if relatedly in other places. The run-up to the US presidential election in 2012 offered another clear, if contrasting, instance for observing how the political theology of race operates.

The political theology of race expresses the ways race colonizes and absolutizes belief. It defines who belongs, who doesn't, who's in, who's out, who has standing in the community, who does not, who's part of the community and who's not, where the lines are drawn, how they are drawn, under what sets of definition, and how those investments become ramified into forms of antagonism, humiliation, refinement, and in some ways rupture. The terms of the theological that resonate can be evoked ...

SSG: ... messianism ...

DTG: ... Yeah, theological rationalizations not only get invoked to legitimate and extend racially ordained social standing; but racial self-assertion itself assumes the "god complex," the self-assertion of infallible power and privilege. I will come back to that.

Looking at the unfolding and operations of race in South Africa, the forms of theological invocation that get mobilized in its terms – you can see this even in Europe – one finds the tension between monogenism and polygenism in accounting for human origins. Are we all – racially – god's children, deriving from one god, or do racially distinct peoples have different origins, undergirding a hierarchy of differentiated potential and possibility on a variety of registers? If we are all one before god, as the sixteenth century would have it, how to account for the differences between us? How is it that some people's skins are stereotypically black and noses flat while others are presumptively white with more pointed noses? What accounts for cultural differences, for differing social arrangements and ways of thinking and being? As polygenism takes precedence from the seventeenth century to Darwin's emergence, the strain of non-godly origin comes to underpin assertions of inherent inferiority, racially conceived. So there are deep resonances of theological doctrine in articulating race itself pretty much from its conceptual emergence, effectively the defining of sociality from the explicitly religious to race as civic religion as modernity was established and got elaborated.

SSG: But you brand that as a kind of separation of race and state. Increasingly, the analogue is in question because the religious separation of church and state seems to be no longer so separate, if it ever was quite so.

DTG: To contemporize, things are now more complicated. Racial differentiation has been increasingly erased conceptually not from the public sphere but from formal state imposition and discriminating practice, from the order of bureaucratic public life. So race is less and less available to use explicitly for administratively regulating population. At the same time there is an intensifying interweaving, if not collapse, between the political and the religious, between church and state, across a range of societies. As there is a drive to centralize religiously identified commitments as state endorsements, racial commitment is displaced from state to private sphere.

SSG: Race evacuation is precisely what fuels the return of religion.

DTG: As religion recedes historically from the bureaucratization of modern life, race enters the picture as a civic religion; and almost 500 years later as racial reference and practice in its name are pushed from the public behind the walled protection of private preference in the name of "racelessness," religious commitment increasingly, if somewhat superficially, shapes and fuels governmental policy. Racial evacuation, as you properly call it, is commensurate with religion re-entering the space of the civic, but in keeping with our time it's a personalized religious commitment, supposedly privatized rather than state-mandated, if abstractly state-regulated or -shaped.

SSG: It's discursively evacuated but obviously those governmentalities are still active.

DTG: So the mode of governmentality has shifted. The formal apparatus of governance can no longer resort explicitly to race as differentiating order. That does not mean that race disappears, as we've seen, and certainly not the effects of race. As it's made to disappear from the formalities of governance, not least by refusing any account of structural or institutional racial ordering, race is protected variously from critical attack or government curtailment in everyday life, in private interactions. Hence the metaphor of racial privacy. Race is not being excised from private life, precisely not. It is being circumscribed, protected from government interference. So people blogging on private sites in explicitly racist terms are protected as expressing free speech. The government can't say to the blogger, "You can't say that." Numerous, but far from all, governments have been reluctant to curtail inciteful or especially demeaning expression, such as "Fitna," the insulting Muhammad video by the awful Dutch politician Geert Wilders, or the Danish cartoons.

The US government could establish grounds to limit public airing of racist expression ("disturbing the peace" has been used successfully to curtail expression critical of Israel, for instance). Yet it has proved reluctant, for political or precedent-setting reasons to do so. In the US, authorities can't say, "You have to be more civil in speech in these and these ways." The blogosphere can express almost whatever it wants so long as it doesn't obviously incite violence. If authorities let free speech flow unhindered, that, too, is a regulatory regime, one that simply hinges on self-regulation and social pressure. Nothing in the First Amendment says society has to provide a forum allowing people to express themselves in racist terms, however. News analysts are repeatedly fired from networks for making disparaging remarks about this or that group because a more heterogeneous public would threaten to take their viewership to less racist broadcasts and advertisers would withdraw. Yet politicians can routinely disparage blacks, Latinos, or Muslims with impunity so long as they are doing so in their own name and not as representatives of the state.

Privatizing renders private racist expression more or less immune. But then to the degree that race is evacuated from explicit expressions of national identity, the religious re-enters as a publicly binding force, a reinforcing of *communitas*. As race became the seculari-zation of the religious, so now it could be said that the religious – styles of thinking and doing, of legislating and conforming – theologizes the racial, reinscribing demarcations of social establishment and belonging. They bind across already racially configured and recon-figured collectivities. Neither the traces nor the exten-sions of race historically understood disappear. They get reinforced actually. They become less touchable, more immune, even less visible until extreme eruptions like Zimmerman's killing of Trayvon Martin, about which the society then says it can do nothing because race wasn't a(n intentional) factor. But they now take on a different resonance with an explicitly theological or re-theologized expression different from what it once was.

You can trace this in different societies. South Africa and the US share similarities in their historical forma-tions, although there are deep differences, too, in their historical specificities. The tensions between a messianic and a missionary tradition – here Boer and British – exactly map onto a distinction between naturalistic and historicist racial expression that then interact with each other, both assertively and critically.

Now these different modalities of race play them-selves out in terms of differentiated "visions" – another theological term, of course. Visions for the future of South Africa and the civilizing mission more or less capitulate to the messianic. Apartheid was a messianic vision: it is a coming, a waiting for that coming, the deferral, a resurrection of a proper place in the world, a fortress against being pariahed ...

SSG: ... and probably anointed, consecrated ...

DTG: ... consecrated actually through memorials like the Voortrekker Monument ...

SSG: ... also blood ...

DTG: ... yes, the Battle of Blood River, the flow of blood, exactly. All those sacrificial gestures and symbolic rationalizations that come also with certain renunciations: We should give up on these things, and ultimately even atone after the fact for these sins we've committed and suffered. Even the post-apartheid Truth and Reconciliation Commission involved atonement, with an explicitly theological resonance. Archbishop Tutu, the co-chair of the TRC, would start and end each of its sessions with collective prayer. So there are lots of theological threads that float through all of this.

SSG: Here's a question you have prompted me to think about often: How do you deal with something buried, alive? Is it an excavation?

DTG: An excavation, an archeology, an exhumation, a digging up to find what's still there pulsing both specifically and in generalizable ways across the national instances, what continues to breathe life into deadly social activities.

SSG: What, then, are the threads sewing together race, political theology, and the erasure of racial terms, their being buried, alive?

DTG: Liquid late modernity increasingly renders explicit racial invocation and reference unspeakable as a form of expression, as an analytic, a comprehension of the world, or an insight into its workings. It's now much more difficult than a decade ago to invoke racial terms, to use them without evoking titters, or prompting dismissal or marginalization. And those most likely to use racial terms are people of color or critical theorists of race in order to characterize the abiding social experience for those not white in modern societies. In dismissal, in tittering, or marginalization, it's again the marginalized and the critical who are caught in double exasperation, a doubling of the condition.

The conditions facing some ethno-racially configured groups have only become more difficult. You are free and equal, but never forget your second-class status, that you are free and equal at the humor of those who have always controlled the terms of engagement, of belonging, of kinship. These complex issues now play into this entanglement between race and racism, the disfiguring of race and the invisibilization of racisms, their unmarking because the terms by which to reference and account for them have been rendered mute. Race is not the same thing it once was, but there's even been a removal of the terms by which to mark these new expressions, to link them to that out of which these new terms have been forged. In struggling to find a language, what gets buried, alive? History: the historical conditions that now manifest silently in contemporary structural conditions.

This burying of the racial manifests in the *absence* of memory, both its erasure and the recursive erasure of erasure, leaving virtually no trace. One can find this at work in South Africa, in the US, where Southern plantations have been turned into tourist attractions, white-washed museums to nostalgic make-believe. (On the far right in the US, and in France for that matter, some are insisting that slavery and colonialism were good for the enslaved and colonized, providing education and culture for the uncivilized which they hardly could have acquired on their own.) In the wake of Israel's War of Independence, this erasure materializes in the complete removal of Palestinian villages and their Hebrew renaming in order to remake national memory through reshaping the lived landscape. The Palestinian village Ein Hawd was remade as Ein Hod, as Susan Slyomovics [1998] and Meron Benvenisti [2000], among others, have so vividly documented.

SSG: These cases do not serve as invitations to think about these issues.

DTG: Precisely not. In the history of Palestine and Israel, any story running counter to the dominant narrative linked to the Holocaust and the founding of the Jewish state is rendered illegitimate because the very terms of counter-narration have been devalued. Saree Makdisi [2010] has written tellingly about this in the attempt to build a "tolerance museum" on the cleared land of the sacred old Palestinian Marmera cemetery in Jerusalem, within sight of the apartheid wall. One cannot escape the intense ironies at work here. A museum in the name of tolerance built on the cleared bones of one's dead enemies alongside a wall constructed to ensure segregation from them. The impact, if not intention, is to isolate the critic, to make her idiolectical, literally speaking only to herself, which, after all, is taken as the sign of madness, of irrationality.

SSG: In contrast to antiracialism, antiracist movements seek to counter what you call the "weight of race" [2009: ch. 9] – a generative metaphor for capturing the heaviness of the racial, how it weighs on and weights down its targeted populations. It offers a more appropriate register of the ways race wears down, insinuates itself into the very texture of everyday lived relations rather than being the occasional frame for one-off episodic encounters so often figured in the contemporary popular imagination, a moment, a short-lived blast from an unpleasant past, a fit of intolerance. The weight of race conjures a more pervasive and persistent presence, a burden to be endured, to be survived. To this end, the weight of race also seems to entail the *wait* of race, as Michael Hanchard [1999] has eloquently elaborated: waiting at checkpoints, waiting for the UN to make a decision, waiting for emergency evacuation plans to congeal, waiting for food, shelter, life-sustaining services, waiting for and wondering if it is the right time for a black president, and so on. Do you agree?

DTG: Waiting is a timely metaphor (pun intended). Its theological dimension is evidenced in its implicit messianism. In racial terms, racial naturalists are waiting for the Kingdom of Heaven, either idealized segregation or the absolutized servicing of those supposed superior by those rendered inferior. Racial historicists are perpetually in waiting for delivery, both that of the historically immature to education, civilization (including Christianization), and self-government and of themselves from any lingering racial guilt.

South Africa for so long was a society in waiting. It still is. Vincent Crapanzano published a book titled

Waiting in 1985. White South Africans – he had in mind especially Afrikaners – were paralyzed by waiting for something to happen, whether for the dreaded apocalypse of black revolution, for the seizing of power by white non-Afrikaners whose principal language and cultural commitments were English, for the dream state of pure apartheid, or more abstractly for being overrun by barbarians at the gate. The sense of utter anxiety, terror, and, perversely, excitement, even incipient desire in anticipation of the latter, all racially prompted or exacerbated, was extraordinarily captured by J.M. Coetzee in his now classic *Waiting for the Barbarians* [1980], arguably South Africa's greatest novelistic writing.

Waiting for the Barbarians poses for us this pressed connection between the politics of resentment and waiting either for some awful apocalyptic coming or for some utopian future. It raises also how in politically indexed conflicts this sense of waiting is deeply racially predicated. The Barbarians are invariably racially differentiated from the "rightful" inhabitants who are in waiting either for the invasion or for a purified state from which the Barbarians are permanently excised.

The projection of a figure of the Barbarian necessarily predicates itself on a self-ascription of civilization and civility. If *they* are Barbarian, *we* are Civilized. And the measure of the civilized tends historically to be racially white – indeed, a purified European. Think of apartheid South Africa, or post-1948 Israel, or the contemporary vilification of Muslims. The paranoia, the fears, the anxieties, which attach and detach then to the self-claim of civilization in the global provinces are a function of thinking oneself never quite good enough to measure up. The provincial European or white wannabe always has to prove him- or herself. It's the typical provincial paranoia.

In that period of apartheid in which the townships were in flames and being rendered ungovernable, whites were reduced to waiting, constantly waiting with trepidation for the deluge, for revolution. Waiting became the default, the state of doing nothing, of passive aggression. South African whites had been waiting for things to resolve themselves, waiting to leave. So the condition of waiting had become, if not emblematic of the society, then constitutive of daily life for whites. For blacks, it was a time of revolution, not waiting. So there was something active rather than passive. That condition being-in-waiting, that way of being in the world, now infuses South African life, often in less tangible ways: one waits in lines constantly, at the bank, at hospitals. One waits for the interminable social tensions to resolve themselves, for the delivery of social goods, compelling education for children, equitable distribution of resources, decent jobs and housing, water, and electricity. Now this is partly having to do with the fact that the service infrastructure – hospitals, the banking service, schools, universities, etc. – was established under apartheid effectively for 5 million people, mainly in service of the white demographic minority (just 20 percent of the population), and now serves roughly 45 million people. All of a sudden there is a reason for many more folk to be at the bank: cashing wages, being encouraged to develop savings accounts, running a business. It is in some ways metaphorical of the waiting that takes place at large: waiting to find parking spaces, waiting at the gas station, waiting for something to happen. Crime is constantly on people's minds, so there is the waiting to get mugged, for your car to be ripped off, or for your house to be broken into, which are all to larger or lesser degrees real.

Policing the crisis is often overplayed in the imaginary, but it has real dimensions. One waits to get work or a welfare check or a check-up; one waits for dying, not least in a society so stricken by HIV/AIDS. Five million out of 45 million people, more than 10 percent, are HIV positive. More than 20 percent of the male population between 19 and 35, overwhelmingly black, are infected. These are all really pressing, enormous concerns. Waiting for dying to eventuate is a real event that many people experience on a daily basis. I think here of Zakes Mda's wonderful novel, *Ways of Dying* [2002] Mario Vargas Llosa remarks, in his compelling biography of the British diplomat Roger Casement, who did so much to curtail the racially fraught atrocities of the rubber trade in the Congo Free State and Putumayo but fell foul of the British as he became radicalized in his drive to free Ireland from British colonialism, that waiting "meant dying many times each day, each hour, each minute" [2012: 301]. Waiting, it could be said, marks time, across different social spaces and scales.

Before 2008 in the US we were waiting for a black president and now we await a female president So you quickly see how we are talking about race and gender. When is the right time? Is there a right time? Are we ready for it? What would it take to be ready for a black or woman president who looks little different from the many white male presidential candidates?

The notion of waiting is also a deferral, a putting off. It is often an exacerbation of the weight, of the burdens that get borne, the deferrals themselves heightening the volume, the pressure, the tension, the disappointment. We were so close and it got pulled from under our feet. Paradise arrived – he won, after all – but it wasn't what we expected, bargained for, worked to gain. Heightening expectations, dashing them, which then fuel the fire of anger and pessimism, lack of hope and disavowal. This is exacerbated, too, by waiting on government indecision, on the self-minded politicking around fiscal sequestration, austerity, government shutdowns, debt ceilings, and the implementation of reasonable health insurance for (almost) all, the waiting on which always most harms society's most vulnerable.

Waiting is not just a metaphor but is a notion to be teased out in different sites under different conditions and has long been related to responding to racial repression. I am waiting for Kingdom come, I am waiting for the day when I'll be able to vote, I am waiting to see a black president in the White House, I am waiting to see my oppressor get his comeuppance. I think it factors into having to live with, coming to terms with, in a way that is a deferral that both enables and disables simultaneously, allows and disallows, makes possible and renders impossible. Is the President black enough? Is he too black? These questions, too, are not unrelated to the phenomenon of waiting and putting off, of the not yet, already.

Waiting additionally signals an ambivalence. This is borne out in the case of Obama, among others, if always differently. Obama may be no worse than anybody else who would have been in his position today, though from one president to another in the last decade there does seem to be a contest of out-muscling the predecessor. Can Obama carry the weight of having to live with all the contradictions of his standing within the body politic? Can he carry the hope invested in him by all sides (at least at the time of his election) or face up to the inevitable fury of disappointment or refusal, both heightened by racial consideration, following the predictable fall from grace? The hope of a black president who isn't black because race is unmentionable, the category snatched away. Is he white enough for whites to vote for him and to put him into power and represent not so much the aspiration as the desperation that he not be something they most fear? Is he too liberal? Is he not liberal enough? Is he large enough to walk away from disasters like Iraq or Afghanistan or Pakistan and leave a mess and yet respond to the mess in a way that is not invasive or inhumane?

Buried in Obama's biography there is added weight that gets born(e). There is a great deal of investment. And investment sometimes leads to divestment, as we have seen. He doesn't trigger the animosity that Jesse Jackson triggered ...

SSG: ... and he is not as easily dismissed as Jesse Jackson was ...

DTG: Precisely. There was an interesting moment when Barack Obama was interviewed on *60 Minutes* right after his first election but before taking office, with Michelle at his side. The interviewer turned to her and asked, "Are you worried that your husband might get shot?" Michelle Obama pithily replied, "He can get shot walking to the supermarket around the corner." Moments of unscripted truth can be so revealing

– presaging Obama's later response that he, too, could be, could have been, Trayvon Martin come home.

SSG: Was she registering him as a black man in public or as anyone ... ?

DTG: No, no, she was definitely registering him as a black man who, like any black man walking down the road, could readily be shot, could be sacrificed to, for, and by white anxiety. That was a very savvy answer on her part, not to mention prescient and honest. For one, it showed her to be a very thoughtful person, somebody willing to cut to the chase, and incisive, and to do it by quietly referencing racially structured social circumstances larger than just him. Those moments emerge out of nowhere, are unpredictable, and yet resonate with lived experience.

A moment of revelation. Given the animus with which Obama's election and re-election have been greeted in some conservative quarters, the unleashing of buried, alive pent-up racisms, there is unfortunately the sense in which the nation awaits at least an attempted assassination, or repeated threats, the fear buried, alive too, and not so deeply.

The other thing about waiting given South African history concerns the relation to the messianic I mentioned earlier. There are these two lines in South African history regarding the political theology of race that are in contest with each other. One is the messianic, linked to Afrikaner nationalism, and the other the missionary, the civilizing mission. Apartheid was projected as the messiah coming. It just did not quite work out that way. The messianic condition arrived only in part, in bits and pieces, meeting resistance on the ground, almost in fear of manifesting itself, of completing its worldly manifestation (*laughs*). The messianic in any case rarely does. And when it does appear, as with apartheid, it is far uglier than its projection. The messianic rears its head, it comes to matter, to be invoked, in the millennial moment. The end of the century, and especially the end of the millennium, somehow conjures the messianic, the end of time. But the end of time also raises the question of what is coming, the expectation, pregnancy, fear, and anxiety that go along with it. Lars von Trier's *Melancholia* spoke quite deeply to this set of relations between the apocalyptic, waiting, fear, anxiety and indeed *white* waiting, privilege, and anxiety, the weight of the waiting of race.

4

Racial states

SSG: Among your more pointed criticisms of contemporary race theorizing is the general absence of any theory of the state. Given the authority of the state to determine who is granted the rights and protections of citizenship and who is denied, who is friend and who is enemy, as well as its increasing concern with policing borders and managing flows of immigrants, it appears to be a startling absence. At the same time, many have claimed that state power is in decline as a result of the emergence of a global economy.

Jean and John Comaroff explain that this is

> why it is so commonly said, many states are finding it impossible to meet the material demands placed upon them by their citizenry or to carry out effective economic development policies; why few can adequately house, feed, school, and ensure the health of their populations; why even fewer can see their way clear to settling their national debt or reducing their deficits; why only a handful can be confident about the replacement of infrastructure over the

medium term; why almost none have the capacity to control their money supply, let alone flows of goods and people; and why a growing number have shown a startling inability to regulate violence. [2001: 29]

Of course, they go on to complicate that picture considerably, even muddying the debates further by asserting that a "strong state" has always been something of a fantasy. How does your conception of the state address these questions?

DTG: I'm not the first to talk about the racial state. Voegelin first explicitly addressed the relation between race and state in the early 1930s (as a Jew, he fled Austria in 1933). His book on *Race and State* is formative and incredibly prescient for the time [1933a/1977], as is his other book on *The History of the Race Idea* [1933b/1988]. Both are extraordinarily insightful contributions to the philosophical study of race, before most everybody else (Du Bois [1903/1962] is the one exception). The term "racism" was first coined, as we noted, by Magnus Hirschfeld in Germany in 1933. Voegelin was seeing something no other theorist was engaging with. Think of the Frankfurt school: it wasn't till after the war that they formatively came to the table in relation to this set of concerns. Voegelin effectively is in Vienna coterminously with the late Vienna circle, as it was dispersing. In relation to questions of logical positivism here in the same intellectual and urban circles, he is taking up a very different set of problematics than they are facing up to. Some of them were of course engaged in socialist politics, but he is making an argument for the ways in which ideas of race are embedded in the formation of modern European thought and state formation that others really would not see for a decade or more as a result of world historical events.

Now Omi and Winant have a chapter called "The Racial State" [in *Racial Formations*, 1986]. It's important that they named a chapter thus, but there is no real theorizing in it of the racial state. They are theorizing racial formation *in* the state. The political struggles over racially inscribed meanings demand more detailed explanation than you find in their book, but even so, there is not a theorizing of the state as it is forged by and through race so much as a theorizing of a pre-formed state that comes to assume or be inflected with racial meanings (even as they assert baldly at one point that the state is structured racially, without showing how so). In their theory in contrast to their declaration, race remains instrumental – in a sense "epiphenomenal" – to the state, rather than constitutive.

I was concerned, by contrast, to open up spaces for productively analyzing the relation between material conditions and cultural expression, institutional power and its articulations. And to do so by thinking about the ways in which state power, as an ordering of institutional constitution, and culture were implicated in and with each other. David Lloyd and Paul Thomas's little book *Culture and the State* [1997] was quite helpful. I wanted to think about the state in this more complex way.

And then, third, there is the book named *The Racial State* [1991] by Michael Burleigh and Wolfgang Wippermann on Nazi Germany. It goes back to an even narrower version of what Voegelin was identifying some sixty years earlier. Given that there was a book already titled *The Racial State*, if I was writing a book just about Nazi Germany I would not have called it that. But as I say in the preface of my book, *The Racial State*, I am undertaking something much larger and I think more provocative than a history of a single state. For sure, the German state of that period is a racial state, even an exemplary racial state. But it was not the only racial state. I was concerned to open up the question in relation to state theory, and to do it by thinking of the state in a more complex way than simply its institutional apparatuses.

The modern state is constitutively formed and fashioned through race in a way which state theory has almost exclusively ignored. When I began rereading the state theory literature in earnest with this focus in mind, I was stunned at how absent any understanding of racial workings was. Bob Jessop [1990], to take just one notable example, wrote a 500-something-page book on state formation and state capital with just a single sentence on ethnicity, and no mention of race. It clearly wasn't simply an absence of talking about race but an absence of thinking the state constitutively in relation to race, which seemed to me basic to the modern, especially liberal, project. States become modern by taking on racial configuration, by constituting themselves more or less explicitly in and through race, not just epiphenomenally but as a structuring condition.

From the late eighteenth century onwards, earlier absolutist states increasingly gave way to modern liberal ones, or so the standard historiography goes. Technologies of population classification, coordination, and management were racially configured from the outset, ultimately pervading state form in the later nineteenth and into the twentieth centuries. Once structured – following Stuart Hall, we should say articulated – in and through racial configuration, a good deal of policy making and many rules and regulations come to exhibit inequitable racial effects and implications, no matter the "intention" expressed by state agents. Modern states developed into population containers, securing people within their boundaries, and after the Great Depression they increasingly offered a safety net for those fully considered citizens. So you have this container state, on one hand, and welfare provider–caretaker state – on the other.

SSG: This speaks to shifting conceptions of state ordering. You've described modernity's obsession with order and with keeping the forces of disorder at bay. Of course, for many social scientists our present historical moment is apt to be described precisely by conditions of disorder, volatility, insecurity, and risk – conditions both manufactured and manipulated by states but also upon states, marking the limits of state power and control. So have we reached the end of the era of modern order, thus entering a new era, marked variously as the "condition of postmodernity" (David Harvey [1990]), "liquid modernity" (Zygmunt Bauman [2000]), or "second modernity" (Ulrich Beck [2012])? If so, in what ways have racial logics or racial governmentalities shifted accordingly?

DTG: There is no question a shift took place, however and whenever you precisely mark its periodization. Prompted perhaps by the radical dislocations of World War II and the surge in globalizing productivity resulting from post-war reconstruction, another deep shift emerged in the 1970s. Harvey [1990] indicates that the petroleum crisis of 1972–3 was an important consideration. By the end of the 1970s, both geopolitical and intellectual shifts were becoming patently evident. The two almost always go together, the intellectual movement – the Owl of Minerva – usually following the geopolitical, to give account or representation of it. It becomes visible late in the 1970s and into the 1980s, even though its elements, the cracks, might have started to appear earlier. Reagan, Thatcher, Kohl, and Pinochet are the obvious global figures embodying these shifts, fueled by and fueling the rise of the Chicago economists, but there are others too. These figures are symptoms of something deeper and larger, and they exacerbate these trends by introducing policies that open up and push along what quickly come to be called neoliberal commitments. Foucault's 1978–9 lectures, "The Birth of Biopolitics" [2008], analyze the history that produces what he is the first critical commentator to name explicitly and historicize as *neoliberal* formations.

Whatever one calls it, whether postmodernity, liquid or second modernity – each of these designations speaks to aspects of the phenomenon – this, then, is also the point of explicit neoliberal expression. Harvey himself has tried to give some specificity to the notion in his little book *A Brief History of Neoliberalism* [2007]. It's a period in which the caretaker state, the welfare state, increasingly comes under attack. Its foundations are cut from under it and it begins to be dramatically cut back as a consequence. It's made to fold in on itself, to implode in a way that leaves the possibility for the emergence and impact of neoconservatism as its political-cultural articulation, which is deeply related to neoliberalism but not the same thing. The declaration that the state – where the state is understood as a set of capacities – will shrink gets enacted through tax reduction, through taking away its means to bankroll these possibilities. This is as much a political as an economic intervention, driven by ideological commitment. The state, considered as looking after people, particularly those who have less means by which to look after themselves, is the state to be cut, which is being eroded, diminished, eviscerated. It is the state taken as increasingly representing the interests of blackness across any number of countries. The state becomes not only the largest employer of blacks and people of color generally, but in some instances it is run by black functionaries. And so the state comes to be identified with looking after the interests of blacks, of people of color.

Each of the elements making up the overall condition being marked by neoliberalization assumes also a racial logic, itself beginning to shift simultaneously. By the mid-1980s, a number of things emerge together. It takes pretty much the whole of the 1990s to produce the effects fully. Tax cuts were being enacted, undercutting the sorts of social programs servicing less well-positioned social members, who tended mostly to be people of color, and a new form of governmentality was being imposed. The 1980s also witnessed the return of vocal *public* racist expression, unashamed in its vocality. Add here the ending of the Cold War rather dramatically in the late 1980s with the series of local revolutions that were fomented from the ground up, and the ending of formal apartheid, which is often not put in play with all of this but occurs in the same period and is produced in part by a common set of forces. The stress on individualization and individual self-responsibility was seen to run up against states ordered in the name of group interests, whether supposedly working class or white.

Formal apartheid was no longer thinkable in a globalizing political economy the modality of which so stresses the individual and unhindered flows of capital (financial and human), goods and services, as well as information flows. A collective agency in the name of a state modality of race was out of kilter with globalizing forces of political economy predicated on flows, individualization, privatization, and financialization. This of course was exacerbated by a political economy that was imploding under apartheid as a result of the townships being made ungovernable by the resistance movement on the ground and the global divestment campaigns, so governing forces were under great duress. The business community in South Africa was up in arms because it was being isolated from global economic interactivity that was asserting crucial impacts even on local political economies.

Along with all of this was a shift across a wide range of nation-states toward trying to defund the state for pretty much anything but repressive apparatuses, for most purposes except policing, the military, and forces of repression, forces for keeping increasing numbers of people of color under lock and key. In the US, the military-industrial complex pulled state prisons into its orbit of operation. Local economies abandoned by closed military bases had to be shored up in new ways. Where they could, some turned to tourism or other service industries. But those with fewer options found their salvation in the prison system, another repressive apparatus. It helped to underpin the political economy by readily transforming the existing military infrastructure – barracks, watchtowers, fenced-off laagers – to site state prisons. This did not replace the military complex but supplemented it as a more individualizing sociality was being produced.

In all, a sociality takes hold that is not about commonality, not about collectivity, not about looking after others, but about looking after, taking responsibility for, only oneself and one's family. For instance, legislation was introduced in the US holding parents responsible for criminal violations their children might enact. While formulated in raceless terms, the legislation was clearly aimed at poorer urban communities of color.

Neoliberalism emerged initially in vocal opposition to welfarism (and of course Keynesianism). Where the welfare state sought to regulate economic activity in the interests of securing citizens' wellbeing, neoliberalism stresses privatization and the (at least potential) financialization of all aspects of life. It's often said that the neoliberal project is out to undo the state. Grover Norquist notoriously once declared that he wanted to shrink the state so he could drown it in the bathtub. But neoliberalism is committed to undoing not the state as such so much as the specifically caretaking functions of welfarism. The claim to drowning the state completely is disingenuous ...

SSG: ... certainly, especially as it grows and grows ...

DTG: ... exactly. The point is less to shrink the state as a whole than to downsize or eliminate specific state functions, namely, those considered its welfare commitments. The neoliberal attack today in the US is on Obamacare, on any publicly funded or managed health coverage, on food stamps for the working poor, on immigration, in the very same breath as insisting on preserving or expanding military and policing budgets. So the neoliberal shifts state priorities, those of materialization, institutionalization, and, most importantly, of whom the state is *for*.

It is crucial to note that the neoliberal attack on welfarism ramps up and takes hold of the public imagination exactly at the moment that demographic heterogeneity expands in leading welfarist states across Europe and North America, in postsocialist states in Eastern Europe, and it is mounted by anti-labor regimes in states like Australia and Chile. Where welfarism had flourished for populations considered racially homogenous, it comes under the knife – perhaps one should say Norquist's waterboard – once the caretaking is seen to have to expand to cover those considered begrudgingly, if at all, to belong. Similarly, the demand today with which EU leaders and the IMF insist on austerity from the deep debtor states of Southern Europe strikes at the perceived bulge of their welfarism, characterizing their populations as idle if not lazy, their administrators incompetent if not corrupt, state handouts akin to those to "welfare queens" elsewhere. The charges are tinged with at least the hint of racial innuendo. The neoliberal attack on the caretaker state is the simultaneous commitment to racial neoliberalism.

In the post-civil rights moment, the state came to be seen by conservatives and whites more generally as serving people of color. Hence the attack on affirmative action, on welfare, on immigration, on refugees, the recriminalization of populations of color, the renewed warehousing of racially characterized non-belonging. You find here the contradiction between refusing race as a state project – the insistence on colorblindness, on racelessness – and reinscribing race as a personally chosen project, which again is a state project because the state shapes the conditions of possibility. And so the attack on the state is on that form of the state identified and expressed in explicitly racial terms. The attack on the state accordingly is seen as an attack on the state servicing black folk, as the largest employer of people of color, as making possible affirmative action, as enabling "welfare queens," as not being tough on crime or illegal immigration. The emerging (re-)emphasis of local jurisdiction – states rights, municipal self-insistence – represents the logic at play here too, as towns or cities insist on profiling policies either to retain their homogeneity or to contain, constrain, and control heterogeneity. So "stop and frisk" in New York City (ruled unconstitutional just as Mayor Bloomberg was leaving office) has overwhelmingly profiled black and brown residents; and municipal localities in Switzerland are banning asylum seekers from public places like school playgrounds, playing fields, swimming pools, churches, or Alpine ski resorts in the interests of supposedly maintaining citizen security.

The caretaker state gives way bit by bit to the more or less openly repressive state, and one is left to fend for oneself. Changes in thinking about race become visibly entangled with these broader social shifts as well. Not only the attack on affirmative action, on the state as representing the interests of blackness, on immigration. I mean all of these things, of course, but also an attack on the very concept of race in the name of government itself. The publicness of racial invocation is under attack even and especially for progressive purposes. Affirmative action, not just in its micro-detail, its micro-politics, but as a symbolic phenomenon, was a flip side, one might say, of anti-apartheid. Apartheid is wrong, racial discrimination is wrong; well, if it's wrong in South Africa, it's wrong in the global North too, whatever purpose for which race might be invoked. The attack on race, rendering race invisible, without addressing the underlying conditions of exclusion and inequality, makes it harder to attack the conditions of racial exclusion and inequality because the mechanisms by which to identify them are no longer available. One can no longer identify the exclusion and inequality as racial for the terms by which to do so have been erased. In actuality, race becomes unspeakable, but unspeakable in both senses of the term.

Ironically, all these things are being articulated, implicitly or explicitly, ironically in racial terms. As the state is being shrunk, it is being prompted to shift its priorities. Numerous things are going on: First, resources are being redirected to technologies and forces of securitization, to repressive state apparatuses, and to tax givebacks, which service what I define structurally as whiteness, those already disproportionately materially privileged. Second, through this privileging of the already better-off, the beneficiaries of whiteness, privatized interests are better positioned to define what heretofore had been the privy of state definition and shaping. Third, these novel modes of privatized sociality sponsor and promote a new driving subjectivity, one centralizing innovativeness and enterprise, self-reliance and resilience, risk-taking (willing to take everything to extremes) and playing hard (gamification), cleverness and cultivated unseriousness, alongside ironically promiscuous deprivatization of personal information, compelling purveyors of make-believe. The rest are just consumers. In short, there are shifts from the primacy of the political to that of the economic, from sovereignty to market supremacy. The Man of Enterprise, as Foucault [2008] calls *him*, centers participatory interaction and social fabrication for the sake of leveraging networks, securing self-advantage, closing the deal, and satisfying passing desires. A new study reveals that the new entrepreneurial class is overwhelmingly white, male, and from privileged backgrounds. The enterprising subject is the new white.

SSG: Your forecast for the future of New Orleans suggests a troubling image for the prospects of cities. New Orleans is an apartheid city returned in the form of sanitized Disney escape, a product of informalized processes of free market "choice" and what you have recently called "born again segregation" [Goldberg 2009: 100]. It is an image of the city that has been a longstanding preoccupation throughout your work, from your discussion of race and urban location in *Racist Culture* [1993] to your latest project *The Threat of Race*, where you describe a process of "racial americanization" in which "homogenized apartness is taken as the deracialized norm, the assumed, the natural, the given," and "[i]ntegration, or at least desegregation, comes over as unnatural, literally absurd, and irrational in the prevailing order of things, requiring intervention by the state at the cost of liberty" [Goldberg 2009: 92].

There has been a great deal of thought recently devoted to the problem of "distance and diminishing duties," to borrow one of your phrases from *Racist Culture*, in relation to the ethical fallout of exterritorialized power, the capacity of capital to take flight while populations remain immobilized, bound(ed) to locality. You are concerned here with the diminished sense of civic responsibility and social justice that segregation inevitably reproduces. Can you address the consequences for the US, a country nominally committed to democracy, liberty, equality?

DTG: Katrina, in 2005, was a moment in which all this became undeniably evident. You could say it leaked out with the water FEMA, the Federal Emergency Management Agency, was incapable of responding effectively because its defunding deprived it of the resources and commensurate training and management to deliver necessary relief in timely fashion. What materialized in the wake was the largest charity-giving undertaking in the country's history – something like a staggering $500 billion. With public agencies unable to mobilize the necessary resources for people at dire risk, who were losing their lives, who were subjected to the most horrendous conditions in a largely black city in the American South, the social response was left to *uncoordinated private* initiatives.

You see here the shift from public to private in on-the-ground responses. The state's role becomes solely to police, to secure the area, to disperse black people, to manage the possibilities of their futures so they don't too readily return. New Orleans was transformed after Katrina from a majority black city, electing representatives who represent their interests and so on, to one no longer so readily black, from a black political elite (Ray Nagin was Mayor as Katrina struck) to the re-entrenchment of prevailing white economic interests (Mitch Landrieu, the newest line of the storied Louisiana political family, is now Mayor). The HBO series *Treme* maps the intricate interweaving transformations taking place along these lines in post-Katrina New Orleans. The moment of privatization, of neoliberalization, of race and the shifting of the priority of the state is materialized by a natural-social disaster.

More broadly, the US is obviously a deeply divided country, in ways both historically shaped by and indicative of the divides facing increasingly heterogeneous countries and cities. The commitment to neoliberal privatization reinforces racisms as personal preferences, as a habit of the heart, as choices individuals make not choices structured by social arrangement, by predefined state possibilities and impossibilities. The US has become a country that in repeatedly committing people to this form of constrained freedom is condemning them in the last instance to a freedom to die. Foucault [2003] cleverly distinguishes between "making live and letting die," on one hand, and "letting live and making die," on the other. The New Hampshire state slogan states the contrast more baldly, in an especially revealing way for neoliberal state reformation that brings together personalized preference schemes with proliferating profiled repression by the state. Live free according to state dictates or you will be made to die, you will be left to die. You won't have an existence worth living. More than "Land of the Free and Home of the Brave," "Live Free or Die" offers a more honest expression of the neoliberalizing commitment, both at home and abroad …

SSG: … an irony you point out when you talk about Operation Enduring Freedom. What kind of freedom has to be "endured"?

DTG: Right, right …

SSG: You are hinting here at implications for thinking about civility.

DTG: *About Schmidt* is a revealing film in this regard. Schmidt was marked by a deep indifference that only gave way to making a difference in his life in order to save his own poverty – his impoverished spirit – from himself. It became simply about himself. Riding an RV (a "recreational vehicle," the name says it all) across America became a medium for finding himself, for coming to terms with his own emptiness, filling that void he could find no other way to fill and turning to giving modestly to charity when he could not be fulfilled any other way. That's a form of indifference actually, of taking distance by relating to the different in class and racial terms at a distance. Touched but untouched. Touched emotionally, but untouched in any meaningful material sense. All those emotionally manipulative MSNBC evening commercials to give to care organizations for orphaned, hobbled African and South Asian kids – airing as they do alongside emotionally comparable commercials to save stray animals – are no different.

Indifference today is expressed in sending record amounts of money to the Red Cross in the wake of Katrina, a tsunami, an earthquake. Some courageous people do put themselves at risk to deliver material assistance in very difficult conditions. But not much changes structurally. Years on after the devastating earthquake, inhabitants of Haiti still await solid housing, clean running water, electricity, sanitary sewerage. But who is paying attention to that anymore in the global North? What is the connection of the civility of charity to the meaningful transformation of the life of those suffering on the ground? Those who do go and try to make a difference in various ways are hugely admirable, and deserve our ongoing support. But for the most part the record giving is momentary. It is a limited substitute for decimated welfare, the privatization of safety nets shredded in the name of individual rights, neoliberal tax "relief," state austerity measures, and the cultivation of personal, individuated resilience. And this sort of giving, in the end, is about the giver's self-salvation.

All this exemplifies for us what is at stake in the move to racial neoliberalization.

5
Fearing Foucault

SSG: The French philosopher and political theorist Michel Foucault has had a significant impact on your work over the past two decades, bookending the earliest to the most recent contributions. His relevance to the study of race was largely untapped until, among others, the work of Stuart Hall, Ann Stoler's *Race and the Education of Desire* [1993], Achille Mbembe [1992], and the translation of the lectures known as *Society Must Be Defended* [2003b]. Foucault's influence is felt in your preoccupation with the discursive deployment of race in the order, distribution, control, and management of populations within the context of modernity. His early archeological work is particularly productive for you in theorizing racial and racist discursive expression as they circulate with startling flexibility across modern discourses of science, aesthetics, history, law, and morality, and the sites at which such knowledges are created. This strikes me as a significant intervention given the ways in which this formulation utterly upends the common sense of racial definition and racist strategy. So I am wondering how your insistence on the utility of a general open theory of race and racism as a discursive field has been met?

DTG: If you look at *theories* of race and racism, they mostly span sociology, on one hand, and philosophy disciplinarily understood, on the other. Interestingly, Foucault's work can be said to speak to both. His reflections on the founding of modern disciplines, the histories of structures of thinking, as he would put it, are revealing here.

Theorists have tended to respond to disciplinary problematics. Philosophers speak to the philosophical questions that drive them: Does race exist ontologically? Does it have any standing as a biological category, referring to something "in nature"? How many more times do we have to see a response to such questions? And as much as I am no longer particularly intrigued by another contribution to the philosophical question "Does race exist?" I have a similar reaction to the sociological version of this that asks, "Is race a social construction?" Is there any credible argument that race is anything other than socially formed and fashioned (as opposed to "naturally" or "biologically" or "physically" prompted), that it is not a biological but a "social fact"?

With respect to both sets of claims, this is surely knowledge we pretty much can be confident in having. Any doubters would be analogous to climate change deniers. Can we start from these points, as some compelling philosophical and sociological analyses of race do, instead of ending there? I grow impatient having to read another contribution to these now traditional questions which were important twenty or more years ago. Unless there is something that is not just new, but new in a big way to say about how these issues should affect us in the world now, why bother? I think here of the really important work of Nadia Abu El-Haj in her new book *The Genealogical Science* [2012], an early draft of which I was asked to read, about the political epistemology of genetic science and the implications for thinking about racial and ethnic claims. A terrifically compelling work. Otherwise the repetition becomes awfully insular, nothing but professionalized self-reference.

Concerning how my work has been taken up, I have been publicly accused of resisting any contributions on the subject not written by or I guess in the language of "Foucault, Derrida, or Agamben." Hilarious actually, this is so not me. There is often a pigeon-holing of the theory: oh, he's the Foucault guy on race, which is utterly reductive, a product in my case of *Racist Culture*. As though there was no pushing beyond those beginnings. Like any range of analysts – Stuart Hall, Zygmunt Bauman, indeed Paul Gilroy and Ann Stoler jump to mind – I don't see myself belonging to any school of thinking, or having a driving need to defend Foucault, even as I am happy to say I have been fueled by his work. I have found Foucault generative, much as Frantz Fanon, Hannah Arendt, Stuart Hall, Angela Davis, Achille Mbembe, and Étienne Balibar have been for me, and it is these generativities that have been helpful in thinking through important social or theoretical concerns. I consider focus on a critical analysis of concerns crucial, not an enamorment with this or that thinker. Foucault himself commented about his trajectory that he was interested in pushing his work to new places, to "becoming someone else" than the thinker from which he began, that everyone had come to expect. That's what I take good writing to be, and aspire to it in my own work, figuring out in and through the process of writing what I actually think about the subject matter in question.

At the same time there have been a range of critical responses to my work over the years. These responses to my general theoretical thrust have come overwhelmingly from those who profess Marxist leanings. I think this largely has to do with the itchiness they feel with Foucault's critical contribution, the challenge to their theoretical frame they sense from it. And they invariably hold me up as the poster boy – perhaps, better, the fall guy – for what a Foucauldian theory of race would look like. These responses have largely been dismal. They tend to render Foucault superficial, to deeply misread what he was trying to do, to miss what I find in and from him.

Foucault has largely been read through a conventional prism as offering a history of race and racism while erasing the possibility of a resistant (some say "revolutionary") subject or social agent. The first sort of view you find in the utterly presumptuous but (at least in some US circles) increasingly widely cited article by Brady Heiner on "Foucault and the Black Panthers" [2007], in which he claims with no credible evidence that Foucault ripped off his conception of genealogy as well as his focus on prisons from George Jackson. The second you find in the likes of Christopher Kyriakides and Rodolfo Torres in *Race Defaced* [2012] and in Ben Carter and Satnam Virdee's "Racism and the

Sociological Imagination" [2008], both of which see me as the Foucault surrogate.

The structure of the latter two pieces goes something like this: Foucault – and Goldberg following him – kill the subject, history's agent. With the death of the subject, any possibility of resistance to racism is killed off. So there has to be a subject, resistant or revolutionary. Besides the fact that this commits a basic logical fallacy – the conclusion is unacceptable, therefore the premise from which the conclusion follows must be untenable – it just butchers Foucault and seriously misreads my own work and how I take Foucault up. But the recourse to an unquestioned stable "historical agency," individual and collective, also trivializes the philosophical challenges both to the question of the subject and to collective action we have witnessed over the past few decades. The shift from resistance movements to rebellious refusals, from what Chandiren Valayden [2013] tellingly maps as that from representational to participatory politics, that have materialized all over of late magnifies the theoretical challenges we now face.

SSG: This notion that Foucault was "killing off" or erasing human subjectivity is terribly reductive, no?

DTG: Yes. Foucault's point was not to kill off the "subject(s) of history," whatever that might mean, but to account historically for the emergence, force, continuities and discontinuities over time of systems of thinking – in this case of systems of racial thinking. And to insist on the historical fashioning of human subjects, to resist some naturalization of subjectivity.

In *Society Must Be Defended* (*SMBD*) [2003b], he limits the emergence of "state racism" to the moment of eugenics and the explicitly "scientific" expression of racism in the second half of the nineteenth century. I think here he is just historically wrong. The early lineaments of state racism start much earlier, arguably in Spain in the mid-fifteenth century, but, in any case, state racism is quite explicit in classification schemes, census taking, and constitution making in the latter part of the eighteenth century. Race, as I have said, constitutionally orders the emergence of modern state formations, structuring subjects as racial, who belongs, whom the state represents and serves, in whose (racial) name it states itself. This perhaps also reinforces the criticism widely and properly leveled at Foucault that his account is so tethered not just to the French archive but to European contours, geographical and intellectual. He fails largely to take account of the fact that France and Europe more generally are made modern, become so, through racially fueled colonial encounter. He thus overlooks the constitutive relationality between the racial making of modern France and Europe and racially ordered coloniality, bi-directionally.

That said, though, the conventional reading of Foucault as offering a history of racism deeply misstates what he is doing in *SMBD*. In references prior to the nineteenth century, he is not so much offering a genealogy of racism – Foucault explicitly says that he is not offering a history of racism in the conventional sense – as taking race as a model of thinking for class struggle, a model logic for the emergent class wars of the period. His analytic use of "race war" and the work it is doing is somewhat different from the meaning given to the notion by George Jackson. The notion, after all, was in widespread use in the 1960s and 1970s. Here, Foucault's genealogy of race discourse (in contrast to what he characterizes as state racism) is really a component of a broader genealogy of technologies of state formation, governmentality, and securing the social. That reveals the deep connection, almost invariably overlooked, between the lectures of 1974–5 (*Abnormal* [2003a]), 1975–6 (*SMBD* [2003b]), and 1977–8 (*Security, Territory, Population* [2009]). It is really only in the latter that he first explicitly elaborates the notion of governmentality.

An aside, but a revealing one. A few years ago I taught a graduate course on "Foucault's Lectures" in which we read all his then available lecture series thus far translated into English, from *Abnormal* to *The Government of Self and Others*. Reading them through chronologically you see a somewhat different development in Foucault's thinking than conventionally understood from reading this or that lecture series or part of his corpus discretely. It impacts both how we read his views on race and race war (in contrast to his much thinner remarks on racism) and how to comprehend his deep history of the "aesthetic and ethics of the self" toward the end of his life. It gives the lie completely to the likes of James Miller's [1994] biographical trivialization and sensationalism.

As for Heiner, he claims Foucault got his ideas for genealogy – which he reads tendentiously and simplistically as the practice of "desubjugating historical knowledges" – and his shift to focus on prisons from the Black Panthers, notably George Jackson and Angela Davis. The evidence he offers is at best circumstantial: Foucault

had helped to found and he wrote some of the pamph-
lets in 1970–1 for the Parisian prison activist group, the
Groupe d'Information sur les Prisons, and had clearly
read Panther writings at the time. (As close as she was
with Jackson at the end of his life, Angela Davis actually
never joined the Panthers, another little unsettling coun-
ter-detail in Heiner's make-believe.) The Panthers,
Heiner says, brought Foucault to Nietzsche and genealogy, and by extension to prison writing.

Where to begin? At the end of his life, Foucault characterizes himself as "always having been a Nietzschean"
(a fact borne out by his doctoral dissertation on Kant's
anthropology). Like all good young transgressives, he
was reading the *Genealogy of Morals* as a teenager, not
simply in 1970. While he doesn't call it genealogy in the
1960s, the section on history in the closing chapter of
The Order of Things [1970] (published a few years
earlier than his turn to reading the Panthers) begins to
lay out the elemental threads of what would become his
notion (and practice) of genealogy. The distinction
between genealogy and archeology that Foucault comes
to draw is in effect his response to the structuralist
distinction circulating in the 1960s between the synchronic and diachronic, and the very reason he so
adamantly rejected the labels of "structuralist" or
"poststructuralist."

On the face of it the claim that the Panthers prompted
Foucault's work on prisons is perhaps a touch more
plausible. But here, too, the history of Foucault's production definitively signals otherwise. The second
chapter of *Madness and Civilization*, which he was
writing nearly a decade earlier, was titled "The Great
Confinement," indicating his longstanding concern with

confining institutional sites and spaces as well as orders of thinking that structure societies in and through disciplinary technologies. Hence his abiding theoretical concern with the hospital, the asylum, the prison, the school, the army barracks, in short with disciplinary institutions. Foucault, after all, was the student of Althusser (remember "repressive state apparatuses," anyone?), and through Althusser no doubt was reading Gramsci, including *The Prison Notebooks*, which had long been translated into French (though Foucault, I believe, read Italian and German). That he could only have gotten the idea for work on prisons from reading black Americans of course also belies what was happening in this regard in France and Algeria at the time, as Angela Davis herself has been the first to point out and David Macey's [2004] usefully detailed biography of Foucault makes abundantly clear.

It's not that Foucault couldn't have been interested in or inspired by Jackson and Davis. He clearly was. But his interest in and inspiration from them were products of the fact that they spoke to interests and concerns that had already been fueling him for a good long while, at least since his days in Tunisia after *Les Mots et les Choses* (*The Order of Things*) was published. Heiner and his uncritical followers rest their case not just on Foucault's contributions to prison activism in France in the early 1970s but also on the fact that his principal theoretical work in the area, *Discipline and Punish*, was only written in the mid-1970s. Yet *Discipline and Punish* is not an account of contemporary penality but a theoretical analysis of the history of penology and conceptions of punishment, based on the French archive (and the influence of Bentham in the shifts attendant to that archive). And this critical concern with confinement and social disciplining dates back to Foucault's earliest work on mental institutions, hospitals, and the production of normalization. In the name of saving history, Heiner and his followers have the historical record completely inverted and the theoretical record thoroughly mangled. There are longstanding interests and experiences among both French and black American prisoners and prison activists (among whom Genet and Jackson, Foucault and Davis rank as most prominent). By the early 1970s the critical concern with prisons as spaces of confinement becomes mutually intertwined.

SSG: Yeah. And that's what I take to be the significance not only of the descriptor "racial" but also of the ways in which you are engaging the question of the state and decentering it, like Foucault. I also think you are not so mired in certain kinds of debates that define the 1970s that he was perhaps pushing to rupture.

DTG: That's right. In this regard, it would also be interesting to read Foucault's reflections on race alongside Stuart Hall's seminal article "Gramsci's Relevance to the Analysis of Racism and Ethnicity," first published by UNESCO in 1985 [see also Hall 1986].

SSG: From *Racist Culture*, the implication of the discursive reach of race is made more explicit in your conceptualizations of what you call "racial governmentalities" – of governance by institutions, by knowledges, by definitions and disciplinary practices racially predicated and motivated in the racial state. Can you elaborate on this conceptualization given the tendency I think

still to reduce the racial state – even hearing this articulation remains relatively rare – to political economy or
to its obvious colonial form? This is often at the expense
of examining how, as you say, institutional governance
depends for its functionalities on the embodiment and
reiteration in everyday practices of micro and informal
expressions of assumed states of being. So by embed-
ding itself in the lived conditions of the everyday, racisms
survive, as you put it, in institutional forms.

DTG: The notion of "governmentality" becomes productive because it has broader applicability, not tied
simply or reductively to institutional apparatuses. Even
while Foucault is thinking of prisons, hospitals, and
mental asylums – things that at least once could be
called state apparatuses but one doesn't think of as
bureaucracies only – both their conceptual frame and
their substance serve to define the form, the logics, the
rationalities, of governance and self-governance. So hospitals and health embed modes, rationalities, of self-
rule. Governmentality runs together the rationalities by
which a state governs its subjects, the ways in and by
which subjects are "made" to make themselves, to act
and behave (in a sense, to be and to have, how we exist,
consume, and possess). But governmentality also
involves the processes by which subjects are rendered as
social subjects, the rationalities of their "subjectivation." Note not simply subjectification as domination,
but their being made subjects. These two senses are
often confused, collapsed, not least in reading Foucault,
so that critics like Kyriakides and Torres (but far from
them only) misunderstand Foucault's conception of
power only as negative, as domination or repression, as

imposed upon subjects, thus reducing subjectivation merely to subjectification, when he explicitly and emphatically draws the distinction precisely by insisting that power also has productive force. Power may be prolific in this conception, but it is prolific metaphysically, so to speak, and not simply as a repressive or imposed condition.

So how does this translate into questions around race? How to think the state in relation to race without simply reducing the state to its institutional apparatuses? A state is a form and mode (or set of modes) of assertion, it's a "stating." And here the Comaroffs [2001] are helpful in thinking through the assertive power of the state in relation to law, how law gets embodied, how subjects take up the law and come to govern themselves in and through law but still govern themselves. It's those forms of regulation and self-regulation that condition thinking about how racial states get enacted, how subjects are produced and reproduce themselves in and through everyday practice. And obviously feminist theory, partly in critical conversation with Foucault, helps in thinking through some of these themes, speaking to the same general theoretical issues but through a different prism, with the two strands in productive engagement with each other.

SSG: Yes, holding on to that discursive line of thought about self- and state formation, I remind my students that the "state" in the term "racial state" is a noun, but also a verb. It is generative that way, performative as Judith Butler uses the concept, and demands a kind of repetition. The formation of the state, like the self, is predicated on linguistic acts, iterations of various kinds that are invariably self-constituting even as they are constantly and subtly shifting ...

DTG: ... right ... and the repetition comes not just through the state apparatus ...

SSG: ... but through subjection itself ...

DTG: ... subjection here as social subjectivation. One embodies it, comes to inhabit it, and through inhabiting it, it becomes habit, it becomes what and how one lives. Its realization being exactly the point: in being realized, it becomes real ...

SSG: ... or routinized ...

DTG: ... precisely. So it becomes everyday practice. The fact that we drive on one side of the road is a trivial example. It is a habit that is shaped and reproduced by a state apparatus, by law, rules, and regulations. An old friend once sent me a critically ironic postcard. The image was of an empty tarmacked highway in desert landscape. A signpost read: "You are now entering the United States. Remember to think on the right" (*chuckles*). Race works in something like the same way. You get molded into habits, into not noticing the fact that you don't have people you would mark as different than you living next door. So even the marking as different, the spatialization of sameness and differences, of homogenization and heterogenizing, come to be inhabited in certain ways. This reveals how everyday practice is linked to state framing, to stating.

SSG: With his explicit theorization of race and state in *Society Must Be Defended*, Foucault's relevance for any discussion of race and politics became undeniable. In the *Threat of Race* you assert that the modern state "transformed, as Foucault said, into protector of the integrity of superiority and more or less purity" of state citizens. "State sovereignty defends itself above all else so as to secure the group, its ethnoraciality, even to protect its purity, perpetuity, and power, for which it takes itself to exist and which it seeks to represent" [Goldberg 2009: 109]. So, as you say, state sovereignty is really racial sovereignty, which historically has manifested itself as whiteness per se. You complicate this line and extend it considerably, but for now can you talk about what you perceive to be the impact of Foucault's lectures, or at least this part of Foucault, on contemporary race theory more generally?

DTG: *SMBD* originally came into recognition in the English-reading academy through Ann Stoler.

SSG: That middle section in her first book, *Race and the Education of Desire*, because the lectures were under legal lock?

DTG: Not unlike Derrida more recently, whose estate, perhaps ironically, is sitting on his archives, so to speak. The grand figures die and everyone wants a piece of the archive. Foucault's got tied up for many years. He was dead set (excuse the pun) against anything as yet unpublished appearing after he died. He reportedly destroyed most of his unpublished manuscripts shortly before he died. Ann Stoler's book appeared the same year, I believe, as *Racist Culture* – 1993. She and I started talking just as the two books were coming out – we knew of each other's work. I read *Race and the Education of Desire*, which I think is actually two books: There is a book on Foucault and there is a book on race, and it's not quite clear how those two projects meet really in the end as a single book. She was the first one, at least writing in English, who went and did the detailed archival work on the lectures in 1973–4 that became *SMBD* (she is a great archivist, after all, as her later work *Along the Archival Grain* [2009] attests), and we first "read" that lecture set through her: those either not reading French or even those reading French but who did not have access to the material. She reads *SMBD* through Foucault's pithy remarks about race in relation to sexuality in the closing pages of *The History of Sexuality* [1978]. This framing leads her to conflate Foucault's conception of race and his notion of "race war" in *SMBD* with state racism.

It was almost ten years later that the English translation of *SMBD* appeared. Reading the lectures afresh, outside of the framework of Ann Stoler, was quite interesting actually because, as important as her contribution was at the time, those lectures could be read a bit differently than Ann did (though those pushing the most recent misinterpretations would be wise to read her again as she properly identifies Foucault's central line of analysis even as she focuses her own account on teasing out Foucault's musings on state racism in the nineteenth century and the implications for thinking about that notion since).

So I think the response to your question is complex in the following way: As I have suggested, Foucault is not talking about what theorists who are at the center of the debates about race and racism are talking about when they talk especially about race. The larger argument about race war, if one reads the lectures outside the parameters of the conventional histories of race and racism, is really about classes. It's not about race traditionally understood, whatever one might mean by that. Foucault is not offering a conventional history of the notions and practices, individual or institutional, associated with those terms. It is about a larger theory of class fighting, class warfare, class struggle, into which racism comes later to fit, as he says, by the nineteenth century. But the examples he gives of the earlier seventeenth- and eighteenth-century struggles are really class fights or struggles, not conventionally understood racial conflagrations. He is using the binarizing frame, the model, of racial antagonism, of racial war and race struggles, of what he calls the "binary terms of power," to characterize the class struggles that come to define the making of modern Europe and in particular modern France so as to challenge the prevailing conception at the time of a unitary notion of sovereignty. He is plugging this model as a system of thinking into understanding the shift from monarchy to absolutism and then to bourgeois rule, and those fights between the bourgeoisie and the emergence from the peasantry into a working class, the proliferation and profusion of social power that is consequent to all this. He is thus seriously complicating our understanding of the history of race thinking, making of this notion of "race war" a model rather than a literal historical account of physical wars between racially characterized groups.

If you think of current applications of Foucault's suggestion, it is analogous to explaining the repression today by the Egyptian military of the Muslim Brotherhood as a "race war." It is a struggle over power by two contrasting groups with competing visions of the role of Islam in the state. And to legitimate the repression, the military and its apologists are characterizing Brotherhood members as violent, troublemakers, self-interested and unmindful of Egyptian common interest, and in more extreme expressions as scum, murderers, terrorists, Nazis, undemocratic, and so on. The "class struggle" or "race war" at play follows a logic of binary antagonisms resulting in the sort of murderous violence by the state and its rationalizations by those taken to be at odds with the state's "proper" way of being. In his account, Foucault is pointing to the logics of social struggles over state power. And he is finding these struggles of the seventeenth- and eighteenth-century French archive mapping onto "race wars." That is truly novel.

If you don't read Foucault in the way I am suggesting, you are caught in a dilemma: because then he is flat-out wrong about racism only appearing in the nineteenth century. And he has to know better because he attended so closely to the archive. *Scientific* racism only emerges fully in the nineteenth century. There are strands earlier tied to the sciences of the day, but they are not the same, conceptually or operationally, as what comes to be identified as full-blown scientific racism in what Hobsbawm [1989] calls the "age of empire." There is, as Foucault would say in good Althusserian fashion, the play between continuities and an epistemological rupture. What is so compelling about his account prior to the nineteenth century, though, *pace* his reductionist critics, is that he provides a frame for understanding the articulation of race with class through a common order of logics, rationalities, and governmentalities structuring the emergence of the modern. After all, he comes out of and never completely breaks with a serious Marxian tradition.

Kyriakides and Torres chide my Foucauldianism for "extinguishing the value of *transcendent* critique" ([2012: 169] the emphasis is theirs). They nowhere offer grounds for the universal principles underpinning "transcendent critique," taking them completely at face value and for granted. Just as the revolutionary subject "must" exist for there to be revolution, so fallaciously there must be "transcendent critique" for there to be critique. *Post hoc, ergo propter hoc.* In their anti-Foucauldian enthusiasm, they both take aim at a widely circulating straw man and fail to take seriously, if at all, the long-standing critique of transcendentalism. In the rejection of *transcendent* principle, it is not that no principle remains possible. Principles, rather, are found *immanent* in the social conditions and situations in which they are embedded. There is no single "solution" to racism precisely because there is no single racism, and certainly no single tradition. You would think that by now the fantasy of utopian revolutionary overthrow would be a touch tempered by the histories of these revolutions' repeated outcomes.

Antiracisms recognize the variety of racisms in their different contexts, and the need for repeated and varied coalitional struggles, as Angela Davis has long insisted, to address the variety in the specificities of their manifestations. There is no quick, singular fix, no magic bullet. Antiracisms necessarily recognize that some abstract principles – of the universal rights of man, of human equality, etc. – while important horizons of idealized aim, will do little on their own to provide *a* "final" solution. Excuse the reference here, but there is a point to be made: The singularity of solution to a variegated set of conditions will fail, radically, for it is predicated on a presumption of purity – of principle, of person – that, as a Panther once famously remarked, is "part of the problem not the solution." Kyriakides and Torres, and those convinced by them, not only trade on unsustainable stereotypes of the views they reject; in their assertions about "revolutionary subjects," "transcendent" values and principles, and a singular solution to the problem of racism, they are engaged in nothing but wishful, and perhaps wistful, thinking.

If you go back to *The Order of Things*, the emergent scientific racism in the nineteenth century is tied to the intellectual movements in the latter half of the eighteenth century: population studies, actuarialism, the emergence of biology, or more broadly the sciences of man. Foucault has helped us to think anew about race, particularly in the wake of the more or less recent return of the politics of protecting purity.

SSG: Yes, this reach for purity, whether as rationalization or horizon of possibility, has long marked at least one dominant strand of the reach for state power across modernity, and of course it is invariably racially articulated. Can you say a bit more about how you see the pulse of purity playing out politically?

DTG: Arguably, there is at the very least an implicit presumption of the virtue of population and perhaps also cultural purity certainly in all racially naturalist claims. If those not "racially you" are considered inherently inferior, they should be avoided either altogether (the absolutist separations of the most strident of the apartheid projections) or in any but structurally ordered arrangements, notably concerning labor. Claims to cultural purity silently mark many if not all racially historicist claims, out of fear that mixing with the "historically immature" may bring one down. Race contaminates, pollutes the body and cultural politic. One sees this most forcefully in claims to want to live with and among only one's "own cultural kind," from Enoch Powell to Thatcherites in the 1980s, from some Tea Partiers to US Representative Steve King. Curiously, Foucault may offer a way here of seeing what a moment ago I pointed to as the racial logic of class distance in the insistence on "not marrying down," of avoiding what Philip Roth [2001] calls "the human stain." So the work of purity and the perceived attendant dangers of transgressing its strictures manifest all over the place. They are at least incipient to all racial thinking.

Now the reach for purity – what I more generally call homogenization – is very much part of what I understand as racial palestinianization. There is a history, deeply associated with the nineteenth-century founding of Zionism, of protecting the purity of Jews, of what came to be named by founding Zionists like Moses Hess as the "Jewish race." For Hess [1861/2012], "race struggle is primal," as he puts it, class struggle secondary. The originating Zionist vision doesn't only resonate with mid-nineteenth-century race thinking but the alarming evocation of race by those founders is explicit

and sustained. In *The Jewish State* [1896/1908], published in both German and English in 1896, Herzl (who
credits Hess for his formative inspiration in writing the
book) explicitly invokes dominant racial stereotypes of
Jews, Arabs, and Turks to drive his argument.

When one points this out, the prevailing response is:
How dare you! It makes people very nervous because,
in addition to the understandably awkward association
with the conceptual underpinnings of the Holocaust, it
brings the founding characterization of Israel closer to,
if not the classic version of the apartheid state, certainly
to its contemporary self-expression. Think of the furious
debate around Jimmy Carter's book on Israel as an
apartheid state [2006], which he was brave to have
taken on but wimped out after he got so viciously
attacked. Saree Makdisi [2010] has recently shown that
all of the foundational pieces of apartheid state legislation – formal population classification at birth and indicated on ID cards, group areas and population
reservations, restricted property ownership, mixed marriages and "immorality," restricted voting rights, etc. –
have been explicitly adopted in the past few years by
the Israeli state too. This comes much closer to establishing Israel as a classically racial state, predicated on
and reproduced through the reach to maintain purity:
from the strictures on intermarriage to the purging of
Palestinians variously from green line Israel and the
establishment of completely fenced Jewish settlements
to the insistence on separate roads for Palestinians and
Israelis in the West Bank. The latter is effected in the
name of securitization, of course, but the underlying
conception and effective implication is a purification
project.

SSG: In the preface to the edition of *The Souls of Black Folk* which marked its fiftieth anniversary – first published in 1903, the commemoration edition appeared in 1953 – Du Bois was reflecting back on the now famous insistence that the problem of the twentieth century is that of the color line. Little discussed is the fact that in the remembrance he amended the pronouncement as follows:

> I still think that today as yesterday the color line is the great problem of the century but today I see more clearly than yesterday that back of the problem of race and color lays a greater problem which both obscures and implements it and that is the fact that so many civilized people/ persons are willing to let go of comfort even if the price of this is poverty, ignorance, and disease of their fellow men. That it is to maintain this privilege men have waged war until today, war tends to become universal and continuous, and the excuse for this war continues largely to be color and race. [1903/1962: xiii]

So already in 1953 he is imagining a perpetual war. Do you agree that there is this deeper problem, as Du Bois suggests, of indifference to human suffering, even at the price of perpetual war, or does the problem lie perhaps in the problem of the very conception of civility itself? You assert, for example, that policing, schooling, and emphasis on legality as modes of social order by the latter half of the nineteenth century came to displace raw physical violence as principal modes of civil and state control. My question is whether it is this deeper problem of difference or invisibility as you map it, or both.

DTG: Undoubtedly both. Let's come back to this because I think there are two questions in the earlier portions of your remarks: the question of politics as war, and the problem of the color line.

In posing politics as a mode of having become perpetual war, Du Bois is presaging Foucault's *Society Must Be Defended*. It is revealing that each, in his own very distinct way, would have formulated this insight in racially ordered terms. Note here too that this is not a case of Du Bois having causally influenced Foucault, Foucault somehow having stolen ideas unacknowledged once again from a famous black American, *pace* Heiner. That picture dramatically oversimplifies the flow and shaping of intellectual ideas. While speaking to different if overlapping histories, both are pointing to the idea that politics has come to engage in campaigns, battles, struggles with strategy and tactics, with weapons and defense, with charges and counter-charges, with taking and holding ground, and so on. The enemy is demonized, in racial terms of alterity and dehumanization, of what Fanon [1956] more or less at the time Du Bois was writing the 1953 preface to *Souls* would come to characterize, for the very first time, as *racialization*.

Now Du Bois's understanding of the color line lies perhaps in the very conceptualization of civility, of who gets to order what counts as civil and who is capable of its expression. Du Bois always saw so clearly what Martin Luther King at the end of Du Bois's life would see too, namely, that race and class are deeply articulated with each other. It is a deep insight that war would get waged perpetually around this configuration of questions. That politics becomes expressed through the waging of war – race war, class war, the war on poverty, the war on drugs, etc. – speaks to both the militarization of the social and configuring civility in racial terms. Race filters the seeable and the invisibilized, in a whole variety of ways. In his more recent insistence on class as the overlooked and more important qualifier of life's prospects, Walter Benn Michaels [2006] would do well to read Du Bois again to understand just how reductive his view is. (You'd think he would have attended to the critical debate in response to William Julius Wilson's *Declining Significance of Race* [1978] to get the point.)

SSG: Talk about confident theory.

DTG: Indeed. The kind of effacement, erasure, that is done in the name of confidence, erasure not just of a corpus of theory but of a 500-year body of history. Not to mention what is now become a mantra that race and class are imbricated with each other, modulated through each other. Where is all that? Yes, we all should be concerned with poverty, but how is it that the rate of unemployment anywhere you look has people of color doubly unemployed in relation to whites? Or take any index of the quality of life: Blacks suffer double the rate of the lack of quality of life compared to white folk – of hypertension, heart failure, stress-related disease, lack of wealth, inferior schools, health care, easy access to healthy foods, etc. How can you not think race-class together, intersectionally, when these are basic facts of life? Of Palestinians today, 60 percent live under the poverty line. And the poverty line there is $2 a day, while the standard of living among Jewish Israelis, most notably those of European background, ranks among the highest in the world. If you think it's not deeply related to the social conditions of race, you can't have paid much attention.

All this, too, is implicated in the racial politics of warring, in the politics of racial militarization that in their own ways Du Bois and Foucault both insisted we attend to.

6

The raciologics of militarizing society

SSG: One of the many fruitful consequences of your theoretical revisions across *The Racial State* and *The Threat of Race* regarding race and neoliberal capitalism as well as repressive and ideological state apparatuses is a more nuanced and sophisticated analysis of the militarization of everyday life, especially in the United States. In contrast to Althusser's distinction between repression and ideology, you suggest in *The Racial State* that "the military is no longer simply ... an exclusively repressive state apparatus. It plays also a more or less defining role for state socialization in regimes of racial patriarchy" [2002a: 100]. So, far from an imposition, militarism offers a site of active identification, of self-making, those "commitments" you spoke of earlier. Can you expand on this crucial insight, engaging the ways in which the cultures of everyday life are both reflective of and implicated in the processes of militarization, from video gaming to the Junior Reserve Officer Training Corps in high schools, to the paramilitarizing of the police, even the militarizing of emergency response

– whether a natural catastrophe like Katrina or pending flu pandemic? And how race structures, and is structured by, militarization, as you conceive it?

DTG: By militarization of the social I mean both an epistemological and an ontological claim. Epistemologically, militarization constitutes a regime of truth and a way of knowing. Ontologically, it amounts to a way of being in the world that is diffuse, which orders states of being, establishes a "habitus," and to which we pay deference by making its socialities, its modes of social being, our own. The tendency is to think of the military, as a product of its defensive and fighting functions, as providing access to employment, training, and social possibilities not otherwise readily available to segments of citizenry positioned through race and class to occupy lower rungs on the prevailing social scale. In these terms the military is seen as an instrumental stepping stone. But as warring became more technologically sophisticated with World War II, it also meant that the less privileged, less well educated recruits, less likely to be white in societies riddled with racial histories and conditions, have been more vulnerable to death in battle because more likely to be in the direct line of fire. In World War I, the officer corps made up of the sons of the British elite notoriously suffered great loss on the front lines. By World War II, this had already begun to change. Increasingly, those less well positioned in society were pressed into battle as "grunts," the boots on the ground, of warring societies, but also as targets of opportunity in societies marked as enemies. Thinking of militarization merely in these terms reduces the logics of militarization to the military as one state agent among others, rather than as socially constitutive. And it just hints at the racial making of the state without comprehending the mutually reinforcing elements of social militarization and race-making.

SSG: Here your work is so richly generative. You point out that governmentality assumes the logic of efficiency – and, again, it's a much more capacious notion of efficiency than any I have seen – which you redefine as "the product of systemic arrangement, of roles and culture, interlocking pieces and schedules, social orders and personal sensibilities being drawn into a tight, containable circle" [2011: 195]. You argue that "[c]onsumption goods and circuits of capital are fused together in militarized mobilizations, the hardware necessary to militarizing capital at once protected and expanded in the face of, despite, but perversely also through exacerbated threats, heightened risk, managed uncertainty. Militarization has become as necessary to economic practice as breathing to life" [2011: 195]. The consequences of this seem overwhelming in their breadth and scope. What are the implications of this transition from state to market sovereignty for notions of citizenship, collective action, common good, individual and social security? And how is race implicated?

DTG: Starting in the second half of the nineteenth, and thickening through the twentieth and into the twenty-first century, especially the last twenty-five to thirty years, the *militarized* shaping of markets becomes evident. It plays a key role in determining what gets produced, what new technologies are created, even what goods become fashionable. The logic of militarization is constitutive of economic relations, forces, and modes of production. This notion of militarization, of militarized thinking, of how we think about approaching economic production, work, and life, proceeds along what I'm marking as the lines of militarized logic, militarized rationality.

In his departing address as US President, Eisenhower famously acknowledged the centrality of the "military-industrial complex" to American power, economically as much as militarily. Implicit here is the relation between the ontological and epistemological ordering of the social. If the 1960s could be seen as a push to regulate repressive social forces and exploitative economic ones, while deregulating (or liberating) social self-experimentation, the push-back in the following decade soon sought to deregulate the economic, while expanding the repressive, the militarizing forces of the state. This included recognizing and expanding the economic power of militarization. Culture increasingly incorporated militarizing expression both into its vernacular – think of the growing unselfconscious use of "interrogation," "shoot," or "fire away" (in presenting ideas), taking turf, taking no prisoners, "explosive" sportsmen, etc. – and expansively into its marketable consumptive goods (fatigues fashion, first-person shooter video games).

As the economic became increasingly deregulated from the 1980s on, inequities abounded and expanded, squeezing out the middle, dramatically expanding the working and non-working or wageless poor. The insistence on militarizing social control became pervasive, expanding police forces, domesticating military technologies and tactics, ratcheting up domestic surveillance in the name of controlling global terror, proliferating racial profiling in policies like stop and frisk (New York)/stop and search (Britain), eroding voting rights designed to disincentivize voting by poorer people of color, and generally devaluing the social contributions of anyone but wealthier whites (recall Romney's dismissal of the 47 percent). Personal wealth generation has become the sole metric of success, securitization the abiding social concern. Deregulating economic investments is entangled with deepening the regulation of social life.

Ontologically, social militarization encourages central social functions to be militarized, at least organizationally. Obviously policing. Small towns in Midwest America now deploy SWAT teams using armored vehicles in emergency situations. Corporations seek to run like military clockwork. Youth brigades. Uniformed workers. Where a social function seems not to function well, "turning it over to the military" becomes a more direct option. Some public infrastructure provision, such as bridges, levees, and the like, falls under military jurisdiction. Policing of urban riots is turned over to the National Guard, concerning itself above all with preventing looting. Most notoriously, emergency relief calls out the military. A question to ask as a consequence is what it means for, what it does to, emergency response; what does emergency become in that response?

One can ask, too, what it is about the culture of military conduct that gets taken up more invisibly, more silently, shaping and ordering our collective social lives, including our work lives. The challenge is to spell out the militarizing logics that mark marketization, the workplace, how work is conducted in the workplace and is morphing along with a transformation in work habits and behavior, and how we work in the wake of new technologies, many of which were prompted directly out of military R & D. Not just weapons, or jet planes, but the telegraph in an earlier moment, automobiles, motorbikes, computers, GPS, now drones, sensors, and so on.

This notion of work and its transformations is deeply indexed in a dual logic, going back and forth between militarization and civil life. And that logic is marked by what I call, giving a new twist to Foucault's terms, both regulation and discipline. Regulation consists in the forces of regularizing kinds of activities, how one engages in those activities across structural conditions of life, and how those are ordered by the state, by capital, by forces of culture, by social relations. They produce a temporality to life, a regularity, a regularization. Social life is deeply marked by the kind of regularization – standing in lines, filling out forms, whatever it is – that is so much a part of modern life, and is produced by a militarized way of thinking about the world.

Discipline is more individualized. Regulation can shape the world with which people interact. Discipline, as Foucault puts it, bores down on the body itself, and does for the individual what regulation does for the more general level of the social. So when you think about management practices, and where they were inherited from, even in the university, these management practices and the production-line capacity on which management is exercised were fashioned and experimented with in militarized campaigns. The very notion of waging a campaign – that doubling of the conception of waging, of receiving a wage, and of waging a campaign, fighting a battle – gets taken over in corporate life.

And so militarization runs very deep, I want to suggest, in the very notion of efficiency, now more so than ever, because efficiency is the term today that has come to mark our work lives and our political structures. The notion of efficiency, central to neoliberal self-conception – we should be efficient, we should rid ourselves of waste and fraud, we should put every last dollar to work in a capacious way – shapes us, regularizes what we do and how we do it. Efficiency comes with a whole structure, an armature, of how life is lived.

SSG: In terms of how they shape political discourse and life?

DTG: It's curious. Apartheid fell in good part because the doubling structures of segregated racial lives that regulated society and disciplined individuals are the antithesis of efficiency. So that notion of militarization, of running one's office efficiently, of getting rid of waste and fraud, of cutting back or cutting out, of running like a military operation, all those rhetorical tropes quickly come back to haunt us. How it marks political life is that there is a deep relation between this logic of militarization, of thinking the social in and through these terms, and the sense that, as I and many others have pointed out, neoliberalization is not about deregulation but about a different form, style, and content of regulation, where and how it's taking place differently, most notably through the apparatuses of repression, the military, the police, and prisons.

These forms of regulation are upped, as business regulation, frankly, takes on a different mode. And it's that marriage of the two – social regulation and individualizing discipline – that drives modes of formalized social segregation, notably apartheid, Jim Crow. They open the way to different registers of racial expression under neoliberalization. Here *enterprising racisms* presuppose individualizing calculation and a disciplining reliant on reproducing a culture of seeking out and insisting on being with "one's own." It's a racism that denies any intention to discriminate or disparage, that apologizes, if at all, for offense taken but never given, thus extending the problem to the target, never the offender. It's important to note that enterprising racisms rest accordingly on structures of segregating regulation inherited from earlier modes of racism that have sedimented into "given" and taken-for-natural social arrangement.

The nature of racism itself shifts. Political life is now conducted through the commitment to identifying and characterizing *threat*. Threat is marked through racial otherness, by non-belonging. Racial militarization amounts to identifying and characterizing threat, making threat *threatening*, producing the threat that it identifies and characterizes; and in putting in place those very structures that are supposed to protect us against that threat. Politics becomes the racial production and reproduction of threat and its containment.

SSG: To extend the latter point, you assert that "[p]ost-Katrina New Orleans ... is simply Iraq come home" [2009: 89]. It's a startling and profound insight. Can you elaborate on the linkages you see between these two moments, Iraq and Katrina?

DTG: There was a report in the immediate aftermath of Katrina about the military contractor Blackwater, which was chased out of Iraq when its personnel providing security for US diplomats killed seventeen innocent civilians. The founder, Erik Prince, later sold the company and the new owners changed its name a couple of times. The rather chilling report revealed that, before the sale, the very contractors who had served as security detail in Iraq were employed in New Orleans, contracted by the Department of Homeland Security and carrying Louisiana law enforcement badges. Their "mission," as they put it, was to secure the city against "insurrection," for which they could shoot to kill. Driving around the city with M-16s at the draw and in unplated SUVs, they were central not to the "reconstruction" so much as the "redirection" of New Orleans. These mercenaries unilaterally took over a set of apartments in the French Quarter, throwing out residents' furniture. Carrying live ammunition, they responded to some shooting that had broken out by shooting back, I think wounding someone.

You see here again the deep connection between privatization and militarized securitization: Blackwater security was protecting the private property of wealthy individuals and corporations. This ties together very clearly the mode of production in relation to Iraq – the privatization of some of the elements of securing politicians and commercial activity – in and through private means by white mercenaries, basically – and the privatization of those functions in a homeland city, to cut to the chase. So I mean quite literally that New Orleans was Iraq come home. The production of democracy in the name of and through militarization sooner rather than later becomes the militarization of democracy.

The second sense in which one can begin to spell this out is in precisely the way in which the defunding of certain elements of the state has an effect on securing the city in the wake of the hurricane – or more generally the securing of the state in the face of natural disaster. This has to do with the way in which certain populations are targeted and are immediately criminalized, in a sense, pre-criminalized. Here privatized interests are defining the possibilities – the institutional and reconstructive possibilities. And this is being fueled by public funding, whether via tax breaks or through tax write-offs, uneven tax refunds, or more direct forms of redirected state funding: money in the treasury or money borrowed into the treasury, money that can then be redirected for a project that hasn't necessarily been signed off on by anybody, let alone by publics. So it's those forms that are tied to my earlier analysis regarding neoliberalism and the privatization of race.

I think there is an extension worth commenting on here. There's been a long history of elsewheres serving as a laboratory for developing forms of deeply racial practice which are then re-imported into the metropole. Once perfected elsewhere, these are put to work under local conditions. In New Orleans a version of this played out before our eyes. New Orleans was being remade as a majority white city, represented by white politicians, funding reconstruction projects with public money for private interests. The use of drones in domestic policing and surveillance would be a more recent example; after all, they are quieter than helicopters. But it is interesting also how the victim in some circles came to be blamed, that black New Orleanians were ultimately responsible for their own demise. This became a common reversal of postracial raciology, as I will elaborate later. If they couldn't help themselves, it was not the responsibility of government to help them out. All the government was responsible for was to secure the city against insurrection, after all. And almost a decade on, as many Republicans are blaming Obama for the dismal government response for something which happened three years before he took office as are blaming Bush (talk about a God-complex!). Any wagers on the political role of race there, anyone?

There is a relation here also to the question of war. War likewise is conducted elsewhere so you don't see it. For Israelis it's in Palestine, for Americans it's in Iraq or Afghanistan. So, it's whitened, white-washed to a certain degree. Even as the injured who come home are rendered invisible ...

SSG: ... or they get institutionalized ...

DTG: ... which is a form of invisibility ...

SSG: ... they are shoveled off to prisons or entombed in debilitating hospitals.

DTG: In South Africa, for all its incredible transformation that nobody could have imagined twenty years on, poverty is rendered invisible and, as with apartheid, one doesn't have to see it. There was a homeless man lying on a bench at San José Airport recently – outside the security area – who hadn't yet been moved along by the police because this is not the space homeless people are supposed to inhabit. One largely doesn't see homeless people at airports in South Africa either. You see homelessness as soon as you drive off from the airport – there are São Paulo or Mumbai sorts of shanty towns all along the highway – a sort of brazilianization of South Africa. But they are rendered visibly invisible. You actually have to look to see them. In the lead-up to the World Cup in South Africa in 2010, the shanty towns on the side of the road from the airport into the city, visibly there for decades, were cordoned off behind a wall so arriving visitors would not be "put off" by the sight when they arrived. On the other side of the highway, on the way out, they had not added a wall, so you could catch a glimpse going out of what you could not see coming in (though international flights from Cape Town tend to take off at night!). But you can avoid looking. And the avoidance of looking is indifference. The structural conditions of neoliberalism make it increasingly possible to be indifferent.

SSG: This presses your point about militarization as a regime of truth, no?

DTG: Indeed. As a regime of truth, militarization authorizes the securing of belief, providing the prism through which the world is dominantly viewed. It is the index of truth-telling concerning what is and is not the case, who is friend and enemy both internally and externally, whom we tolerate and who is to be held at arm's length, whom strategically to cultivate and whom to write off, whom implicitly to trust and who requires profiling. So in very simplistic ways, just to mobilize the thought, in the decade after 9/11 on every newscast one would find a military commentator discussing security concerns or terrorist groups, the conduct of this war or that. (In the age of sequestration and budget austerity, the discussion has turned to budget cuts and military readiness.) If the economic imperative is to deregulate financialization of everything, the social imperative is to regulate militaristically, to monitor and surveill, to reduce the social to strategies and tactics. Each imposes metrics of calculability. Curiously, the central trading desk, the central command of the trade, at major Wall Street trading firms today is affectionately known as "the turret," or sometimes as "the war room" or "operations room."

These modalities of thinking and seeing become the arbiters of belief, the warrants of truth, of what is and is not the case, what you can or cannot believe, of available data, perhaps even of what constitutes data, of where you can or cannot go, and so on. Every time I travel on university business, I receive "security alerts" from my university about the area to which I am traveling, ranging from flood or other weather warnings to urban uprisings and terrorist events. This militarization provides the indices of how one is or is to be in the world. You can criticize a war in Iraq but you can't criticize the soldiers. They're defending our liberty, after all, even if killing innocents. You can "have your fun" debating state surveillance programs, but when you are told to stop you had better do so or you will be detained and actually interrogated, at length. So this militarizing logic becomes a way of defining a liberty that needs to be defended perhaps because it is not sufficiently perspicacious for others to resonate with them.

The claim is not just about the defense of liberty. It is also about the form that liberty takes, what can and cannot be done, who can and cannot do it, where you can and cannot go, in its name. I would suggest that this is a regime of truth and a way of being in the world the contemporary genealogy of which we can trace to Israel, which has provided the model. Here race is silently key in positioning and rationalizing the targets as not belonging, as terrorists, as vermin, and so as the dispossessed (to use Judith Butler's [2013] term), and discardable. They are simply in the way of utopia, of perpetual peace. But perpetual peace is maintainable only by the perpetuation of the threatening, the barbarian, the philistine. The utopian is always a horizon of possibility, in perpetuity. The point is never to reach it but to keep it alive so as to be able to blame those preventing its realization.

If 9/11 changed anything, it made militarization of the social more evident, more prolific, more global. It divided the world between those who buy into this regime of truth and those who oppose it. It becomes pervasive, for example, not just in the ideological or expressive or discursive form that video games take; it's pervasive in the very production, the mode of production, of those video games. For example, there is a group that has met weekly for some time in Santa Monica, California, consisting of video game makers in the industry and military people who advise each other on the forms the games should take. On one hand, this is in order to make them more realistic so kids ... kid-like people ... can get off on them and, on the other, this is so that they can be used as training technologies for the military in preparing their forces for new modes of techno-combat. A good drone operator is also likely to be a good video game competitor, in response time, in eye–hand coordination, in effectively negotiating the peculiarities of virtual landscapes on a video screen and console. It imparts new meaning to "imaginative geographies." Not to mention the distancing effect that renders guiltless the pushing of the button that launches the drone missile more than likely killing innocents at a distance, even while targeting the bad guy. The militarizing version of racelessness. This has not protected drone operators from suffering post-traumatic stress disorder at rates more than comparable to killing face-to-face. So these technologies have quite deep material purchase on the imaginary in various unpredictable directions.

Another thing about video games. For two decades now, combat and war strategy games have constantly looked to create threatening figures as embodiments of the evildoers. These have almost invariably consisted in what are imagined to be ugly figures with animalesque features, like Orks, and invariably shaded brown. They also draw on images that mimic Pliny's monstrous peoples. Sometimes the racial coding is explicit. One example among many would be the "tau subrace" figures from roleplaygateway.com. Good guys, including warrior women, are rendered white. So the color symbolics plug into stereotypes dating back at least to the Greeks.

SSG: Can you point to specific historical examples where social militarization and race-making explicitly come together?

DTG: There are the obvious cases of the segregation of military units. But these are probably the less interesting instances today. You'll recall that the development of IQ testing, after its initial invention by Binet in France, was fueled by army tests with an explicit racial index in the US during World War I. That testing quickly became widely socially adopted, with deep socio-racial implications.

There's another fascinating example, largely undiscussed, which speaks directly to the articulation of race with social militarization. In 1933, George Fletcher MacMunn, Colonel Commandant of the Royal Artillery in India, first formulated a notion of *martial races*. Perfect example, no? Martial races are the distinct subset of "natives" (MacMunn is focused on India) considered ready for military service. They are trustworthy enough in strength of body, character, and judgment. In short, martial races are those MacMunn considers either open to missionary conversion or sufficiently embodying Christian-like virtues to carry out the ruling imperatives in the face of death-producing war. Interestingly, among Europeans – he explicitly mentions England, France, and Germany – martiality is a natural characteristic of the population at large. "Guts," as MacMunn puts it, is a sort of national character. Among Indians, by contrast, martial races are a small sub class. Only Sikhs and Gurkhas have the requisite courage and judgment. So for Europeans these are birthright qualities, breathed in the cultural air. For non-Europeans, these qualities are taken to need nurturing, training, sustained cultivation. Racially naturalized for the former, racially historicized for those so disposed among the latter.

Thinking more broadly, one can recast the notion of *martial races*, giving it a more extended critical sense. Martial races are both militarized and militarizing races, taken to join raciological and religious character, "manliness" and "loyalty," sovereign judgment and sacrifice, individualized privilege and independent power, honor and a fighting spirit, the transcendental capacity to recognize and defend the racially registered and theologically grounded right and the good. Martial races supposedly embody and enact warring masculinities not simply in military campaigns but at all times, turning everyday life into battles, campaigns, crusades, even fights for survival. They readily sacrifice, in the end even their lives, for the good not just of the nation but of the team, the corporation, the institution, the family, the state, even the race itself, whatever extension that is taken to have. The ultimate form of militarizing citizenship is that of the "sacrifice" – for God and nation. Serving (in) the military, especially in a society not requiring conscription, is a giving up, a giving to kin and country. Conscription is an imposition, an obligation; joining up is a sacrifice, a "free" commitment, freely chosen out of honor or duty.

We find embedded in the definition of this or that "martial race," sometimes only implicitly, the standards set for being a more or less full-fledged member of the society, a social subject with standing. Members of the martial race are leaders even when led, bearers of social responsibility but with privilege. Presumptively white, structurally or aspirationally so. Here, not only do martial races "wage" war and peace, keep order and control the agenda. They "color" the social, shape and "color in" its sociality, shading its sensibilities and sensitivities, what is thought – its convictions and commitments – and what can be expressed. The militarization of the social both reflects and reproduces "militarizing races." It is of course also intensely masculinist.

SSG: Yes, I want to ask a question about women in relationship to the military. In *The Racial State*, you offer a compelling analysis of the tightly knotted relationship between race and gender within the context of nineteenth-century empire. "Colonizing," you write, "was considered man's work, the work of white man's regulative control, to be exact" [2002a: 90]. You describe the colonies as "male clubs of a kind," "a bachelor's paradise," as Helen Callaway [1987: 19] put it.

So whereas "[c]olonization ... was about European men teaching their like to be men, to do men's work, to exercise power and to serve country, ... king ... , and God," white women, as "the bearers or symbols of too much moral conscience," were "admitted to the colonies only begrudgingly" [Goldberg 2002a: 90–1]. Without denying the benefits white women enjoyed as a result of European imperial missions, you suggest that

> because of these preexisting forms of gendered domination on both shores of the colonizing ocean, ambivalence surely marked colonial relations between women on each side of the racial divide more deeply than it did the dominant master–slave relation between white men and black people. European women, it is safe to say, engaged in a less totalizing, more tenuous embrace of whiteness than their male counterparts. [2002a: 91–2]

Thinking about your comments in the context of the United States' expanding imperium, its occupation of Iraq in particular, it seems that women have been all-too-willing conscripts in the war on/of terror. On one hand, the population most against the war, and yet proportionally the most overly represented in US military ranks, are black women (in fact, you note that a full third of the US military is African American). Obviously, there are pressing economic reasons for that. On the other hand, I'm thinking of the two specific women who have come to symbolize a very different reality: National Security Advisor turned Secretary of State Condoleezza Rice and of course Lynndie England, one of the women indicted for her role in the prisoner abuse scandal at Abu Ghraib. I'm wondering if and how you might revise this earlier assessment of the race/gendered dynamics of European imperializing missions to address the racial and gendered complex of today's military?

DTG: Yes, good critique. On one hand, these are clearly different historical moments ...

SSG: ... yes, absolutely ...

DTG: ... and they produce different possibilities. In Israel, every Jewish-Israeli citizen is conscripted into the army for three years in the case of men, two in the case of women. One's social standing as one goes through life in the society is in quite direct ways – not completely, but largely – tied to one's experience, positions one had, in the military. Those occupying the most appealing military positions in Jewish-Israeli eyes are air force pilots and those who occupy senior executive positions in the intelligence service. And if you look at the people who occupy important political positions in the history of Israeli society, they almost all rose through the ranks to generalships and to other senior posts especially in these areas. In a society that increasingly defines its regime of truth through militarization, you can expect that women, in terms of making equal claims and so of having equal access, will have to make their claims through those forms of institutionalization.

I don't want to make too much of that point, but it resonates more broadly. Whether straightforwardly in the military or through those forms of political engagement with it – National Security Advisor, Secretary of State, ultimately possible candidate for the President of the United States – the trajectories of political life are deeply tied to forms of militarization, either directly and explicitly within the narrow institutionalized life of the armed forces or through the politicization of their standing.

On the flip side, two points. One is that we have seen a retreat of the post-9/11 drive for more boots on the ground, for an imperious military and governing occupation of troubled places. All of this has been tied to race, of course. The missions in Iraq and Afghanistan were driven by a sort of racial historicism: we will show you how to govern yourself. The intense masculinization of invasive rule was accompanied by equally intense moments to emasculate and humiliate local men, represented most clearly by Lynndie England and her accomplices in Abu Ghraib. One sees here, as you suggest, the deep articulation of race with gender. There have also been some almost silenced reports of US military men raping Iraqi women. And this then registers also the

127

recent focus in the US on the rabid sexual harassment by men not only of women but also of other men (roughly half the 26,000 sexual harassment instances annually, including rape, by military men are of other men – pretty staggering figures overall, seventy-five or so in total per day). Militarization clearly has a sexual culture, much as colonialism did.

The other point is that, conversely, one shouldn't lose sight of the fact that terrifically progressive and productive forms of not just critique but also social mobilization, social movement, have come out of women's movements. I think of women in Argentina, of the role of women in South Africa. This, of course, can go in a variety of ways. I was, as Cornel West [1994] would say, hopeful without being optimistic that a form of resistance might emerge in relation to expansive imperialisms of the kind we've been witnessing more recently that possibly could emerge from mothers ...

SSG: I was thinking of Cindy Sheehan ...

DTG: ... Cindy Sheehan being an obvious case in point. Facebook's Sheryl Sandberg got a great deal of buzz around her corporate "lean in" campaign (she has since taken a huge hit for seeking an unpaid young woman intern). Rachel Maddow, who wrote a compelling book about war [*Drift*, 2012], is associated with a more progressive "lean forward" strategy. These are corporate celebrity leanings. The Dreamers have largely been led by young dynamic Latina women, as, too, Voto Latino, the voter registration and leadership organization I am now working a little with. In a more coalitional dynamic, is there a way for young women to lead new social media movements to lean away from social militarization and into more compelling progressive political engagements? Demilitarizing democracy will necessitate also a transformed gender politics interactive with an antiracist – a postracist (and not just postracial) – one.

7
Migrating racisms

SSG: You ended your remarks about militarization with a hint at the politics of immigration in the US. What similarities or differences do you see between rising anti-immigrant sentiment in the US and across Europe? Just as there have been ongoing challenges to multiculturalism in the US (and recent laws banning ethnic studies), multiculturalism is largely seen as a failed project in Europe, as Angela Merkel concluded lately. Philosophers such as Jürgen Habermas and Slavoj Žižek see such rhetoric by mainstream politicians as the most expedient way to hail voters who might otherwise drift rightward. In fact, in an editorial in the *New York Times*, Habermas [2010] suggested that the greater concern (and one emerging from altogether different motivations) is the "growing preference for nonpolitical figures on the political scene," which signals for him "the rejection of political parties and party politics." Žižek raises the similar concern that there is now, more and more in Europe, a big liberal capitalist party – no meaningful demarcation between right and left anymore

– and "anti-immigrant nationalism" is the only voice of perceived authentic protest [Žižek and Goodman 2010]. Do you agree with these assessments? Is this kind of "repoliticization in the name of depoliticization" the more grave concern? Is the growing racist animus merely a ploy or distraction? Is it unconnected to this shift in political culture?

DTG: These questions require some historical context. World War II was arguably the first really global war. Compare the respective maps of participants in World War I and World War II. There is a notable expansion with the latter; no one was untouched by World War II. The world was deeply unsettled; migrations magnified dramatically. Europeans and Asians sought to escape the devastation; colonial subjects reached for opportunities in the metropoles, asserting status and the right to metropolitan citizenship in the wake of their own sacrifices to victory. The subsequent waves of decolonization further extended this movement. Labor shortages in the face of post-war reconstruction-fueled production were an additional pull. Presumed homogeneity gave way to much more robust demographic diversity pretty much everywhere, leading to a recognition that perhaps things were never as homogeneous as they might have seemed prior to the war.

This restructuring economically and demographically was exacerbated by the turmoil of the 1960s, in Europe no less than the US, magnified as much by the anti-colonial independence movements as the civil rights, anti-war, and student movements. If the Americas, South, Central, and North, have long seen themselves as immigrant countries, it was really only by the close of the 1960s and into the 1970s that migrations came to harden pejoratively into "immigration," a sort of settling in, troubling the taken-for-granted European sense of self-identity. Enoch Powell's notorious "Rivers of Blood" speech in 1968, ultimately costing him his cabinet post in Britain's Conservative government, was the first vocal register of the push-back. But it was as much these movements of people as the new technologies and flows of capital that manifested in what we have come to recognize as globalization.

The politics of neoliberalism that came to grip the 1980s, in Europe not unlike the US and Latin America, heightened conditions giving rise to rapid movement, from Eastern Europe into Western Europe, as a result of the failures of the Communist Bloc, and the shift from the global South to the North, with folks looking for better living conditions, dignified work, and life opportunities. The push and pull into the North and out of the South soon gave way to a less singular directionality, with people going back and forth, sending remittances "home," the very designation indicative of a lack of permanence, as much in sensibility as materially.

Through the 1970s, this movement from East to West and South to North underpinned the emergence of the multicultural both as a marker of growing demographic diversity and as a set of policies for "benignly" recognizing its cultural expression. While the demand for labor was keeping pace with migration, there was relatively little contestation; these migrations had not yet become robustly contested as "immigration." Citizens of the former colonies were regarded as if "returning" to the metropole – Surinamese in the Netherlands, West Indians in Britain, to a degree Ethiopians in Italy. In

Germany, labor needs were pulling in Moroccans and Turks. If not exactly an openly welcoming passage – Germany until very recently insisted on citizenship being reserved for those with "German blood" – receiving countries still defined themselves as hosts, and sought accordingly to extend hospitality (with some limiting qualification) to the newcomers.

Recession, once again, brought this up short, if not to a screeching halt. By the mid-1970s, the growing visibility of people of color and cultural mixture was increasingly viewed as problematic in European public consciousness. Jobs were drying up, more difficult to find. Cultural difference was seen as rowdiness, the presence of the racially alien as criminal threat. The recognition that "they" were here to stay shifted discourse from migration to immigration, and with immigration to repatriation. That latter notion itself signals non-belonging, the lack of commitment to homeland, to a patria impossibly theirs. Scapegoating for hardship leads to blaming the more or less newcomers for taking "our" jobs, for being willing to work at lower rates. Claims of criminalization kicked in with a policy bent and bite, as *Policing the Crisis* [Hall et al. 1978] captures so well in the case of Britain. Sus (suspicion) laws, on the books since the 1820s, were invoked on Britain's streets to enable police to accost youth of color at will. So multiculturalism as state policy provided cover for more repressive practices. State (in contrast to insurgent) multiculturalism became the institutionalization of tolerance, always expressed from a position of power. These repressive regimes in the name of tolerance did not go unresisted, as Rock Against Racism and SOS Racisme in France, among others, attest.

Into the 1990s across Europe, people of Muslim descent, long present, were made more problematically visible: Pakistani youth in Britain; Moroccans and Algerians especially in France; Moroccans and Turks in Germany and the Netherlands; and so on. They were the targets of disaffected white working-class youth who blamed those they saw as not properly European for their own dwindling opportunities and the former's cultural non-assimilation. Stirred up by the renewal of right-wing political parties across Europe, Muslim youth also became increasingly radicalized. The radicalization was related additionally to more global forces of disaffection in the Islamic world, especially among young men, prompted by lack of opportunity, Western belligerence, and Israeli intransigence regarding Palestinian possibility.

All this became concentrated within the cultural sway of multiculturalism. The descriptive characterization of multiple cultural inputs and expressions for which multiculturalism is a shorthand is tied also to a softish normative commitment regarding demographic cultural and value heterogeneity, a commitment hiding deeper social ambivalence. One has to read all of this against the backdrop of Europe taking itself as "European" since the fifteenth century as an increasingly coherent and homogeneous commitment and identity, having seen staring in its face a radicalized heterogeneity that it was totally incapable of facing up to and negotiating. This sense of "European" is purposefully ambiguous: European as inhabitants of the geographic space of Europe, and European as the metonym of racial whiteness and cultural Christianity more broadly, even globally.

It's this set of forces and structures that became entangled in the 1990s, and was reinforced by 9/11 and by 7/7 in London and the Madrid bombings. While the very notion of "fortress Europe" goes back of course to the 1980s, it gets reified in the wake of these events. Opening up the inside of the continent and closing off its exteriority has been a familiar project, implicit perhaps in the very logic of the notion of Europe itself, from the mid-fifteenth century. So the exclusion at its founding moment of blacks, Moors, and Jews returns, half a millennium later, in the guise of extending black and Muslim exclusion. Jews, by contrast, have now become, because of the Holocaust, at least somewhat less uneasily the mark of Europe's conscience about itself. Jews also "reveal" a Europe a little more heterogeneous than when their absence or expulsion was deemed comfortable, their current acceptability (relatively speaking) tied, if ambivalently, to their sourcing of Christianity.

Habermas [2010] is right, then, that the nativist drift of mainstream parties across much of Europe has been with a view to cutting off the drift of the electorate even further rightward. Race invariably becomes a key factor in the political calculus of modern states. (You could say the same about multiculturalism as the policy position of liberal tolerance.) Žižek characteristically overstates the logic at play, though there is not untypically a keen observation buried in his sometime theoretical bombast [Žižek and Goodman 2010]. The old left and right have become right centrist, overridingly projecting themselves – itself, given Žižek's logic – as the voice of centrism after all: "We represent society, moderation, reasonableness," however reasonableness is characterized. "We're open to gay life, in fact, they're part of us; we have a reasonable sense about gender, so we're completely open to a woman being prime minister," and so on. So our liberal-mindedness, our reasonableness, and our moderation are represented in that articulated set of commitments.

Contrast this with the angry expression, "They're taking our jobs, they're invading us, they're turning Europe into not-Europe." This sort of dismissive projection of immigrants as invaders and thieves represents 15, 20, or 25 percent of the electorate in many European countries today, from neutral Switzerland, vacillating France, to the more left-leaning welfare states of Sweden and other Scandinavian countries. It's not unpredictable that the anti-Muslim cartoons came out of Denmark, that Pim Fortuyn, Rita Verdonk, and Geert Wilders would have emerged as key political voices in the Netherlands, that Jörg Haider would have risen in Austria. And Germany, which has been very careful in the wake of World War II, now feels itself distant enough from those horrifying events to allow itself to begin speaking quite openly and more volubly about the country's loss of a sense of itself, as indicated by a string of recent books from very mainstream German political personalities. And it is not unpredictable that the conservative Swiss People's Party in the 2007 election would have metaphorized its campaign in a widely circulated poster of a white sheep kicking a black sheep out of the country. Aggression parading benignly in the hard kick of a soft boot.

Proponents of this politics of anti-immigration have not fully embraced the language of invasion, but it might as well be the term they would readily use.

Multiculturalism, the claim goes, has failed. Both Angela Merkel and David Cameron have read its last rites, signed the death certificate, and buried it, all in the same breath (and both, ironically, in Germany). Not that it was ever really tried with great vigor; it was managed, top-down, the hosted tolerated under duress and subject to an abiding presumption that *they* should become *us*, rather than that *we* should change *together* and create something new in an interesting, dialogic way. That would have been too much to ask for.

Both Habermas and Žižek are pointing to that transformation which is now quite obvious. It is, as Habermas insists, the sense of protesting uncomfortable change, a way in which protest manifests, both directly against the perceived transformation of visible conditions – after all, protest is the visible mark of the transformation – and, though less noticed, as symptomatic of these other changes. The howls of protest against immigration and immigrants are the expressive equivalent of the "Tea Party of Europe." It is the angry expression that "we're losing control of our lives." This presumes, of course, that "we" once had control of them. The presumptive racial homogeneity, which accordingly needed no articulation, underpinned the implication that we all knew who each other was, or at least could predict how each would act. "We" had control over what our streets looked and behaved like, on what counted as civility, what could be expected walking to the corner store. That sense of lost control has taken on this racial expressiveness in relation to immigration, as the outside, the not belonging, the not being. Anger at this loss is channeled into the more extreme rightist parties across Europe, which is what

Žižek points to as the authenticity of loss, alienation, and dissatisfaction these parties help to express politically. What he fails to attend to, though, is that just as the Tea Party in the US has been orchestrated by wealthy operators, so Europe's "tea partyish" equivalents have been molded by charismatic political characters in whose name they have sought to elevate their own popularity and, by extension, political power.

This politics of contested loss – of deep social dissatisfaction and alienation – eventuates in comparative deprivation and dispossession, the loss of familiarity and control, on one side, and that of the economic left behind, the loss of home, on the other. The question is how to turn the politics of mutual if differentiated loss and its attendant irritations into something else, a politics of collaborative co-making to address not the loss so much as the basis of its production, taking aim at the causes rather than the symptoms, effects, and affects.

The pressing question here becomes how to help each other's societies, across these presumed cultural differences. Could the various parties produce a critical engagement around these questions where one is more directly paying attention not to the projection of an outside coming in and transforming "us" from without but actually to the changes happening from the ground up, which are deeply politico-economic and cultural in their constitution? And to begin to address the sense of loss, which is a sense of loss also for those who are always projected as coming from elsewhere even when locally born and bred, for at least a generation or more. Those actually hailing from elsewhere are leaving behind something, coming to a place they thought otherwise than it is, another sense of loss. How do you put these into conversation with each other, so that the focus of analysis is the multiple, interactive, reinforcing losses *and* gains, and a vision of how these can and do transform into something mutually creative, together? Until we do that, at least more fully, we're going to have this very fierce set of oppositionalities, and the liberal position of trying to find the middle ground is just hopeless, because there really isn't any.

In the US this plays out through the politics of immigration, where the claimed center representing itself as the voice of common sense insists on heightened border security alongside a path to citizenship for the 11 million or so largely Latino illegal immigrants. Tea Party intransigents take only the first stake in the formula, insisting on repatriation and heightened security when faced with, for them, the nightmarish impossibility of preventing any non-authorized migration. The consequence is the knotting of militarization and the Wall.

The fantasy that 11 million can be repatriated (or might "self-deport," as Mitt Romney put it in a presidential primary debate), despite most having longstanding lives in the US, making a productive contribution economically and culturally, and paying taxes, is driven by the racially ordered imaginary of non-belonging. That imaginary is supplemented by the refusal to acknowledge the economic dependency on Latino labor to subsidize low-cost social benefits from ensuring delivery of goods to supermarkets, gas station services, construction site contributions, and so on. And it is shored up by the fantasy that a border wall will condomize the society from illegal access.

SSG: You see the wall, then, as a racial technology?

DTG: Yes, an exemplary one …

SSG: How so?

DTG: In dividing off, political walls are intended by design to mark off the belonging from the non-belonging, the desirable from the undesirable, citizens from threats. Walls are built as interventions in the politics of existing antagonism, but serve to cement them, to harden the categorical distinctions and divides, exacerbating the antagonisms they were supposed to diminish and deepening resentment by splitting families. Political walls shape and fuel the tensions, projecting as raced those who are – or supposedly should be – on the other side of the wall. That supposition that those among "us" ought not to be already undermines the wall's effectivity. No matter how much wall there is, it always requires more: longer, higher, thicker, but also supplementation by policing, surveillance, technological supplementation, ultimately drones. So there's always the political economy of walling. The wall on its own can never suffice. This is also borne out by the fact that walls, rather than being absolute barriers – which, after all, would fly in the face of neoliberalizing flows – shape movement and commerce rather than completely restrict them. Like condoms, walls leak, break, split open through use. They invariably have access points where cheap goods and low-cost labor can come and go under the watchful eye of the seeing state. Designed to divide off the threat from the citizen, the political wall inevitably undercuts its very premise.

One small statistic illustrates the kind of logic at work here. The number of privately sold guns entering Mexico from the US is around 10,000 annually. There is one licensed gun shop in Mexico, run by the military. So 80 percent of all guns, the high-tech weaponry being used in the drug wars and the killings which are proliferating throughout large parts of Mexico at this moment, are not just made but bought in the United States, and easily carried across the border with no questions asked. And there's great resistance on the part of the National Rifle Association to changing how the sale of weapons is policed. These aren't just hunting guns – they're "hunting people" guns, they're military weapons, semi-automatics and the like. This, too, is the logic of militarization.

More benignly, but in ways equally undercutting the categorical distinctions between those who are and who are not citizens, large volumes of produce from Mexico are delivered to (super)markets in the US by a huge trucking fleet driving "through" the wall on a daily basis. The wall is porous in all sorts of ways. The point of political walls is not to prohibit flows but to shape them, to regulate and order and route them in ways conducive to state and economic benefit.

SSG: I want to shift, relatedly, to a question about the Muslim in the post-9/11 racial configuration of the US. A similar logic of regulation and retribution extends to Muslim citizens in America as to Mexicans, or Latinos. Polls in the US over the past half decade have indicated that 39 percent of Americans would have Muslims in the country carry special forms of ID and fully a third view "Muslims as terrorists and breeders of hate." You have described a talk show host in Washington, DC, who baited his studio audience by suggesting that Muslims in the US be branded with a forehead tattoo or forced to wear armbands, recalling Nazi impositions on Jewish citizens of Germany. You write, "The audience responses were shocking, repeatedly calling for exporting [Muslims] or placing them in concentration camps. At show's end the host, himself Jewish, admitted to staging the call for identification marks, strongly chiding the audience for being like fascists in Germany during World War II. A revealing moment" [Goldberg 2009: 94]. But what does it reveal for you, nearly seventy years after that war's end?

DTG: Another quick anecdote, revealing something relatedly. I was contacted by a journalist from the local newspaper, *The Orange County Register*, in Southern California. The newspaper had just started a Community Board response to articles they publish where readers could email in comments. In response to two articles about crime in the area, they received a huge array of responses. The first article was about a foiled assault and attempted rape. The perpetrator was caught and the paper published his name, which was in a way unplaceable: He could have been Farsi, Mexican, or Jewish, for all one knew. The report did not mention his racial background, only his American citizenship. The man, in his mid-20s, had apparently attempted similar assaults earlier. The second story concerned a mugging of an 82-year-old woman coming out of the bank and stealing the $700 she had just cashed. Silly to cash that amount of money and walk out of a bank, not least for a lone old lady. They did not catch the perpetrator, and the report described him in very neutral terms, without ethno-racial characterization.

The Community Board responses overwhelmingly, if not exclusively, urged that the *Mexican* perpetrators be expatriated to Mexico. Explicitly. The language of exhortation was not just candid but also colorful. There was additionally a class resentment apparent in some of the retorts to the initial responses: to the more liberal comments, "Oh, you must live in Irvine" (which is more upscale), "You don't live in the trailer park down in Huntington Beach." So some very interesting and revealing responses. There's a violent history in the US of confusing Sikhs with Muslims, and conflating brown-skinned people generally with Mexicans, or the Mexican border as the entry point for Muslim terrorists (for which there is absolutely no evidence). That "fear of barbarians" about which Todorov [2010] has written. The presumption of who is "us" and the paranoia about a projected "not-us," the bearers of terror, drugs, generalized crime ...

SSG: ... the "not-you" ...

DTG: ... yes, the "you" in the "not-you," a projection or imagination of oneself which likewise licenses one to do or say almost anything, including quite vicious things. Around the same time as the newspaper exchange, young Muslim families in Orange County expressed deepening concern over having to run an organized gauntlet of verbally violent insults at a mall while taking their children to a doctor's appointment or shopping at the supermarket. Scarfed mothers and children were subjected to humiliating verbal assaults, bordering on physical violence, simply in the conduct of their ordinary daily routines.

This connects to the point I was raising earlier about authority and authorization of truth and truth-saying – what can be said, how it's said, who says what to whom, the general condition I call "make-believe." Make-believe is both making things up, and making believe, a compulsion, compelling one's own belief as much as that of others. So force becomes a condition of the production of truth. That of course is linked to the militarization of regimes of truth. The Muslim as generic figure of terrorism exhibits the interactive senses of fantasy and compulsion, licensing restriction, recrimination, repression, extradition, to the point of violent and criminalizing responses. Even universities – my own included – have responded to open critical expression by Muslim students and faculty (usually about Israel's treatment of Palestinians, or relatedly supporting the "boycott, divestment, sanctions" movement) with disciplinary action, sometimes to the point of filing criminal charges against Muslim "perpetrators" for "disturbing the peace" while exercising their free speech.

Modes of truth making and their protection from and compulsion in others are thus deeply connected. What, then, is the index of truth? Who's saying what? How is truth created, fabricated? This establishes a social fabric of make-believe, a fabric of fabrication. People become licensed and license themselves to say whatever. Mitt Romney's "etch-a-sketch campaigning" – what Obama humorously called Romnesia – represents the condition taken to its extreme: Publicly and loudly proclaim something more reasonable than the extreme claims one is known to have made previously and then immediately withdraw the more moderate claims quietly, as if no one will notice that one's real position is the more extreme one.

Such claims are especially amenable to racially driven expression, not least because race itself is constitutively a form of social fabrication. Birther claims that Barack Hussein Obama was not born in Hawaii but outside the US are shored up by the fabrication that he is a Kenyan Muslim socialist anti-colonial, obviously not American, and therefore ineligible for the Presidency. No amount of evidence to the contrary undercuts the fabrication – everything we know about him points to his having been born in Hawaii to an American mother – for the fabrication is grounded not in fact but in an ecology of dismissive belief, a disposition of denial, an epistemology of deception. But in any case one has to ask why such claims even arise for the first time in the case of a presidential candidate, and ultimately of a president, of mixed African-American heritage. In Italy, Cécile Kyenge, the first black cabinet minister, in addition to commonly having bananas thrown at her in public forums, was likened to an orangutan by Roberto Calderoli, an Italian senator. That he called her up to apologize does little to undercut the public humiliation and racial undermining of her authority. In both kinds of cases, race becomes the surrogate of insinuating immigrant non-belonging.

The grounds of such claims are different from traditional truth claims where evidence purports to determine their truth or falsity. And so the response to them must differ too. You can't say, "Well, such and such is true and that runs counter to the claim," or that "He or she is an authority who has offered evidence to support the claim," because all of those things now are up for grabs. Nor can you say, "Well, you said just the opposite the other day," because in claim and counter-claim no one can keep track of all the assertions, no one can keep straight what has been said. Claim and counter-claim come to be inscribed with equal epistemological value.

Take state insistence on outlawing the veil or hijab, namely, the covering of body, face, and head. Note that the claims are formulated "neutrally," to apply to anyone covering up, or in France's case using any head cover. There is a longstanding tradition in which this stands, not least in France. No one, including millionaires, can sleep under the Paris bridges, as Anatole France famously put it. And no one can cover their heads or cover up. But everyone knows that, like paupers sleeping under the bridges, it is Muslims who are being targeted by these new laws. In the name of *laïcité*, one could just as easily have a universal law that frees everyone to wear whatever cover they wish, or none at all. Race operates here through a mode of group anonymization. Curious, isn't it, that the very logic of anonymity for which racial thinking has been discredited is now applied to produce the socially desired effect to prohibit the cultural practices of the racially conceived targeted group?

Outlawing the veil is fear of the cover-up, so to speak. Not the rationalization that "we can't see their eyes," so much as the resentment at having women's bodies hidden from view, unresponsive to look or lure. The veil denies the capacity of anonymous men to look, lasciviously or disdainfully, at any body they choose. But racisms are always about future generations, about

reproduction, about the constitution of the social tomor-
row. So, at least by implication, racisms are always
about – targeted at – the youth. Resistance to the veil,
then, is not just about Muslim women; it is more generically resistance to Muslim reproduction, especially
about not wanting more Muslim men around in the
future. The constant threat of extradition, at the policy
limit, insinuates that there are no inherently good
Muslim men. A doctrinally violent religion – which one
is not? – always holds out the prospect of violent transgression. The only solution, on this logic, is to extradite
or lock up all.

SSG: In the war on terror, racial profiling has been rendered legal, as you point out. The detainment of "enemy
combatants" in Guantánamo Bay, a term used to cir-
cumvent direct violation of the Geneva Conventions,
has also been rendered "legal." The recourse to legality
– to conflating morality and legality, the moral universe
of totalitarianism – produces what Hannah Arendt
[1963] calls "thoughtlessness." I've always found her
analysis here compelling, if problematic, particularly in
light of your work, underscoring the ways in which
reason and not just instrumental rationality can be said
to collude with racism. I wonder how you take Arendt's
notion of "thoughtlessness," because we would like to
think that this is the absence of any kind of direction,
but actually it might not be.

DTG: Just to complicate this a little bit: It's easy to call
racist expression thoughtless. In some cases the responses
to the newspaper blog were thoughtless. Where do you
even begin to respond? Citing counter-figures goes

nowhere. We want to say there is no reason at work, but there is a kind of instrumentalizing reason. One needs to grapple with its instrumentalization and the effects it produces. So one can't just dismiss this as reductively thoughtless, for failing to confront this directly leaves it to reproduce itself.

Thoughtlessness assumes many expressions. In the US, fear of Asian economic dominance produces backlashes, sometimes violent, against Asian residents, now the fastest-growing immigrant group, while often effeminizing Asian men and eroticizing Asian women. Sikhs from time to time have been violently attacked – on the street, gathered at gurdwaras – confused with Muslims and so terrorist, as though attacking Muslims has any more legitimacy. The attack on ethnic studies in schools and universities you mentioned earlier is aimed today, if differentially, at both Middle Eastern and Latino studies programs. In Arizona any teaching of Mexican American studies or history has been outlawed on the claim that it promotes resentment toward whites. No credence is given to the counter that explicitly outlawing Mexican American and by extension Native American histories is born out of and reinforces resentment toward Mexican and Native Americans. Similarly, Middle Eastern studies has come under attack because it is critical of Israel or American foreign policy. Sometimes the attacks are expanded: Extreme supporters of Israel, some of them holding teaching positions at the University of California, have repeatedly filed complaints with the Civil Rights division of the US Department of Education against various UC campuses for creating or tolerating a hostile anti-semitic environment toward Jewish students and faculty as a result of allowing any expression at the university critical of the state of Israel. Thorough investigations in every instance have thrown out the charges. The Texas state Board of Education, dominated now by Tea Party radicals, has just insisted on redefining the school history and social studies curriculum to call the "slave trade" the "Atlantic triangular trade" in the attempt to strike slavery from American history and memory.

One can see here the instrumentalization of thoughtlessness, thoughtlessness as, in, and through these sorts of instrumentalization. Thoughtlessness becomes a mode of instrumentalizing and institutionalizing racist presumption, its presumptive fabrication as common sense ...

SSG: ... or as Arendt seems to be driving at, because it is legal, there is no problem. You are just dutiful ...

DIG: ... the bureaucratization of the effect, which is exactly what I mean by its instrumentalization in a more extended sense. It becomes tacit, mechanical, rote, an instrument, the way in which we think our lives in the everyday. It is thoughtless in exactly this Arendtian sense regarding Eichmann and the banality of evil. This is what I'm used to doing and there is no need to think about it, so it becomes common sense. The default common sense concerning illegals crossing the border is clearly that they should not. We don't care about their biographies, or what produces the need to put one's life at risk in order to wander across, what material pulls there are in terms of subsidizing an affordable lifestyle for the mass of US residents ... Who cares? They are illegal. It's thoughtless in that sense as well. And then the instrumentalization kicks in: If they are illegal, what must follow in order to prevent them? So "we" had better build a wall or a fence, increase the National Guard presence at the border, deport more and more of "them."

There is thoughtlessness, then, that produces different forms of instrumentalization which carry out an effect that is a function of the thoughtlessness, the roteness, the commonsensical, to begin with. Thoughtlessness calls forth instrumentalization, which in turn reinforces thoughtlessness. The premises, the prompts, are thoughtless but they conjure conclusions in syllogistic practical reasoning, the effects of which are troubling. Thoughtlessness cements the absence of any critical or self-critical reflection. It produces and reproduces confirmatory citizens. Thought – critical self-reflectivity – requires us to think back through the syllogistic reasoning ultimately to question the premises "thoughtlessly" taken on at the outset. The critical responses prompting differentiated instrumentalizations, by contrast, are various. They can be violent or transgressive, civilly disobedient: Do you give the illegal immigrants clippers in order to clip the fence, compasses for direction, water in order to get across the desert, a ride when you see them struggling through the daytime desert heat or night freeze? Do you provide sanctuary in churches? Do you hire them as day laborers, to do home construction, or to take care of the kids or the garden not just because their rates are less expensive but also because their work is of higher quality? How to use the Wall not merely as technology of enclosure but as a screen for critical disclosure, as a surface for critical political inscription of the politics of walling as such?

These are different counters, some of which, while instrumentalizing, nevertheless are not reductively so, and thus are necessarily "thought*ful*" by contrast. You are in the US, remember *not* to "think on the right" but to think critically, thoughtfully, not to take the given, the tacit, the commonsensical, for granted – and to act accordingly. That requires a whole lot more effort, because it requires thinking against the grain.

8

Civic lessons

SSG: You have been pulling so many strands together. As we move now to think about contemporary racial articulations in the United States, can you take a moment to rehearse your general theoretical line of argument?

DTG: I have been arguing that what falls under the banner of neoliberalism represents a series of profound social shifts: deregulation of economic forces alongside hyper-social regulation, in a sense economic libertarianism and social disciplinization; intensified privatization, proliferated financialization and marketization alongside dehistoricizing comprehension, narrativized fabrication, and intensified class distinction; and a purging of racial conception and configuration from public institutional order while intensifying the private expression of racial arrangement and racist exclusion, humiliation, and delimitation, all this publicly protected while silencing the terms even to recognize their racial dimensions and expression. The recent emphasis on austerity – globally as much as in the US – has been taken up as a not so blunt instrument to cut more deeply at the caretaking structures of the welfare state, rationalized as the cause of spiraling state debt. In the US, austerity has served less obviously as a technique by which to distance the contemporary polity from historical recognition of society's racial debt. Here the neoliberalizing state is as much a radical retreat from post-1960s civil rights commitments as it is from post-Depression welfarism.

SSG: How so? Can you spell this out?

DTG: We need to read together the principal developments of the last three decades regarding institutional racial arrangements resulting from the civil rights successes in the US: the attacks on voting rights and affirmative action alongside rapidly and massively expanded incarceration. So the rolling back of political and educational access for racially identified populations, notably blacks and Latinos, and the scaling up of criminalization, prisons, and intensified social marginalization [see Wu 2013].

Affirmative action to address desegregated educational access was legislated into being with the 1964 Civil Rights Act. The legal counterattacks started immediately, ratcheting up with a case in 1973, reaching the Supreme Court in 1978, ultimately upholding the possibility of affirmative action so long as it is not diminishing opportunities for white students while adding opportunities for students of color. The attacks on the principle were ramped up in the 1980s under Reagan, were held somewhat at bay under Clinton ("mend it, don't end it"), intensified again under Bush the Younger, and have retained their intensity since, not least by insultingly tying Obama to its legacy as an affirmative action candidate, both educationally (Columbia, Harvard) and politically. An "affirmative action baby," as Stephen Carter's awkward [1992] book title once put it. The Voting Rights Act (1965) legally protected voting rights, persistently resisted especially for African Americans, in the face of widespread constraint by white politicians and their supporters, particularly but not only in the South. The Act required those states with long histories of voting discrimination and racially driven restriction to seek pre-authorization from the US Justice Department for any legislative plans to alter local voting arrangements. Resistance started at least as quickly as it did in the case of affirmative action, involving attempts to restrict or undermine voter registration campaigns, intimidation at voting sites, even literacy tests neutrally worded but aimed exclusively at black voters [Berman 2013]. So there is a long, persisting legacy of educational and political restriction targeting African-American advancement.

The third and most debilitating leg of post-civil rights racial governmentality concerned the rapid expansion of criminalization, incarceration, and the prison industrial complex. The prison population in America spiraled from 200,000 in the early 1970s to a million plus in 1990, and well over 2 million today. Numerous forces come into play together to produce this dramatic increase. Deindustrialization began already in the late 1950s, sped up in the following decades, and, as we know now, was really dramatic. Black workers employed in the manufacturing sector, which promised middle-class prospects, found work more difficult to come by.

Manufacturing gave way increasingly to the emergence of the information economy, which in turn helped to deepen class bifurcation in America. Relatedly, post-Reconstruction urbanization of black folk ultimately intensified urbanization of the racial poor, marginalizing them in cities abandoned in the 1960s in the processes of white suburbanization and capital flight from the central city. In time, this became a new form of suburbanization, producing self-governing entities, small towns, diminishing the tax base of cities that were increasingly black and brown. Detroit's bankruptcy today is a historical legacy of these processes, not to belittle also persistent mismanagement there. The effect of all this was a re-segregation of America through suburbanization [Vanhemert 2013].

The crack epidemic of the mid-1980s, as many have revealed, prompted intensified criminalization from 1984, establishing mandatory sentences as the norm, catching other less pernicious drug offenses in its web as well. Sentencing disparities for crack and cocaine offenses – the former considered a black drug, the latter white – further "blacklisted" the prison population. At least two-thirds of the dramatic increase in incarceration since the 1980s has been for non-violent drug offenses. This, too, became a mode of warehousing the urban poor. In 2008, one in three African-American men without a high school diploma between ages 20 and 34 were behind bars (one in nine of all black men in that age group). For comparably aged white men, it was one in eight without high school certification (and one in fifty-seven for all). These processes helped to produce a surplus population, socially abandoned and warehoused by the criminal justice system, all but disappeared by the state from social concern. A surplus the state no longer cared to care about, let alone care for other than to make invisible. Of no value, it could produce economic value – surplus value – only through incarceration. Neoliberalism refines both the processes and rationalizations of this social enablement.

Prisoners present and past were denuded of voting rights, robbed of civil standing. Unemployable, stripped of political voice without voting power, powerless economically and politically, black men especially were abandoned by the state when not buried in the cement and wire cages of the carceral state. Michelle Alexander [2012] has compellingly called this "the new Jim Crow" [see Thompson 2013].

SSG: The annual cost of a prisoner is more or less $30,000. Multiply that by 2.3 million and the annual cost of US incarceration is close to $70 billion. While these expenditures don't quite equal the war on terror, they represent a less acknowledged war on people going on now for decades. These costs have helped to bank-rupt some states in America. So while some may be talking about cost efficiency, you have the most expensive means for dealing with crime – the most wasteful economically and personally, humanly. This exacerbates or hastens the destruction of the social state; but it also heightens violence. It becomes part of a self-strangulated state condition.

DTG: The costs are staggering, in human and economic terms. As conservatives in the country insist on the heteronormative family as the moral standard bearer of successful sociality (this in a nation which sees 50 percent of marriages ending in divorce), they actualize policies that absolutely destabilize family life for people of color (debilitating prison life for black folk, deportation for undocumented Latinos). Families are torn apart, children cut off from parents. California today spends more on its prisons than it does on higher education. There is, of course, a correlation between education and avoiding prison.

Crime is not some "natural" condition, those misleading studies about genetic codings for crime notwithstanding. The spiraling figures since the 1970s have been extended by "stop and frisk" policies, whether formally in New York City or informally in cities across the country. In New York, until the Supreme Court recently declared it unconstitutional, 650,000 people annually were being "randomly" stopped by the NYPD. Nearly 90 percent of those stopped, "walking while black," are racially profiled black and brown people, including South Asian and Middle Eastern men, despite the fact that the racially indexed crime rates – produced in good part by this policy – are considerably lower. Something like 12 percent of stop and frisks violate some law, usually marijuana possession, almost never illegal weapons. A black or brown person is stopped literally every minute, every day of the year in New York. "Look, Mama, a negro," a Muslim. A New York terrorism squad also targets mosques for intrusive surveillance. Implicit racial profiling of Muslim networks in the proliferation of National Security Agency [NSA] surveillance can be read as virtual stop and frisk. So what counts as crime and who gets criminalized are deeply embedded in a society's political and cultural economies, one could almost say in its social DNA.

A little-known history connects prisons to militarization, dating at least to the post-1987 US recession. Military budgets under Bush I were trending downward, resulting from the recession and a recognition of shifting post-Cold War notions of technologically enabled defense and warfare. Bases were being closed, and local economies centered on them were under duress. A significant part of fixing this was tied to the prison-industrial complex. As military bases were closed, their land and building infrastructure were offered to the Bureau of Prisons. President Bush wrote to states offering them these bases – in Arizona, in the California desert – for a dollar. Prisons were quickly established on those sites at a nominal cost to the states, using the existing infrastructure of barracks, kitchens, fenced perimeters, and so on. There's a shift back and forth between the military and prisons as a regulating apparatus for warehousing surplus populations. Prisons become militarized infrastructures.

We could telescope ahead fifteen years regarding Abu Ghraib and the offshoring of this condition. There was already in the 1990s the global commercialization of these apparatuses and technologies in the name of prison marketization. South Africa began to purchase American technologies of criminalization. The annual association meetings of the crime control industry involved above all the marketing of technologies of policing and prison control. These gatherings amounted to industrial exhibition, wholesaling of available technologies: digitized ankle locks so that people could be followed around, implants ...

SSG: ... tasers ...

DTG: ... new forms of handcuffing ...

SSG: ... electronic surveillance and electrified razor wire ...

DTG: These technologies cohere as "an industry" in the 1990s. First perfected in places like Angola, the notorious Louisiana prison, and in supermaxes like California's infamous Pelican Bay, they are unleashed on the world. Prisoners in Pelican Bay are all in solitary confinement around the clock. They get one hour of exercise time a day under caged conditions, otherwise they are locked away in single cells with no human contact, no sunlight. Even their food is delivered through special openings to avoid human interaction. These are the most horrendous, dehumanized and dehumanizing conditions. When a prisoner starts acting up in his cell, a special unit goes in to bring him out, to "extract" him, as the technical term puts it; the extractive unit is militarily trained. These technologies – the carceral and the military – map onto each other and are prefaces to militarized adventurism. The practices and technologies get exported elsewhere, at first secretly, invisibly, experimented with elsewhere, and re-imported – until slips and mistakes make them more visible. This connection between the emergence of the prison-industrial complex, as Angela Davis [1998] would name it, and the militarization of prisons deepens social militarization, as I characterized it earlier.

SSG: On the flip side, this signals conceiving what constitutes a citizen, a civilian, in military terms. In talking about criminals, rights are eviscerated, especially, though far from only, in the private prison context. The insistence today on the concept of "enemy combatant" does similar work. These terms now render the distinctions much more fluid, if not quite meaningless. Is what emerges out of this newly configured political economy an instance of what Mbembe [2003] has called the necropolitical?

DTG: It is indeed a sociality predicated on managing death in new ways, on mandating death and on abandonment resulting in avoidable death. (Think here, too, of the debates around universal health care in the US, and, among large segments of radicalized Republicans, the disinterest in, if not refusal of, health care coverage for anyone incapable of covering themselves.) So death and its management become the very condition of the political. It is a politics in which death is a principal technology that not only disciplines, those calculations by the self around living life so as to minimize risk, but regulates, the management of heterogeneous populations, of the social itself. In his important essay "Necropolitics," Achille Mbembe [2003] is obviously talking about a different, if related, range of effects of this exercise of power over life and death, of who gets to live under what conditions, and who gets to die, most notably under conditions of war-making in the colonies and in the postcolony. He does not take up an analysis of prisons explicitly, but what I have been describing here clearly fits his account.

Loïc Wacquant [2002] stresses the arc from slavery through Jim Crow and urban ghettoes to the carceral state as a racially produced linearity, if not itinerary.

There is something to this, identifying the racial not only as common thread but as the driving condition of that arc, the archeology of the social in the trajectory of American history. Wacquant is especially concerned to identify each moment in that arc with renewal of extractive labor practices. That said, his historical linearity fails to address the specificities of racial articulation at different moments across American temporalities. There is no focus on what forces interact with the modes of economic extraction but also sometimes at odds with them to produce different racial conceptions, understandings, social arrangements, and political outcomes at different times. He does not address how race serves to articulate new trajectories in the political economy and governmentality of the state from one prevailing moment to the next. Nor is it really meaningful to say that the US is the first carceral state in history – what of the Gulag, of apartheid South Africa? I have been suggesting that the drive to criminalize and incarcerate in the US is a driving piece of a larger logic of militarizing society, in which racial conception operates in various ways – informally renewing racially discrete cities, hyper-inequities, gated communities and incarcerated populations, criminals and terrorists, failed states and enemy combatants, invasive surveillance and repatriated non-citizens.

SSG: You enumerate various strategies employed by Republicans to discourage black voters from showing up at the polls, or even registering. One of the most successful strategies is the manipulation of felony disenfranchisement – and more recently the felonizing of specific crimes, like infractions committed by protestors who transgress the constricted spaces now assigned to them in which to take such action. These examples proliferate not just across cities but also on college campuses. The denial of black voting rights central to George W. Bush's 2000 "win" of the Florida electoral college and recently the Republican campaign in 2012 are obvious instances. Marc Mauer and Meda Chesney-Lind's *Invisible Punishment* [2011] argues that seven senatorial seats in the mid-1990s were won this way. Most striking to me is the likely durability of these informalized exclusions, which seem far more resistant to legal challenge than formal Jim Crow policies. It's difficult to imagine where the popular will to challenge the disenfranchisement of both felons and former felons would emerge in such a retribution-driven penal context. Yet such exclusion undermines not just black political representation, but the integrity of the political system in general.

DTG: The production of these complexly configured arrangements has to do not just with the marginalization of prisoners but also with their rendering almost as nonpersons, and so with their invisibility. The prisoner has no rights because he – largely, though we also have the spiraling of women's incarceration, which manifests differently, if relatedly – has ceased to be a civilian. Not just a citizen, but a member of a society.

SSG: Socially dead.

DTG: Yeah, the production of social death. Regarding former felons, the very notion of rehabilitation has been eradicated as a possibility, as a programmatic response.

But its demise is also linked to the refusal to register the felonious person's life as worthy of any recognition. It's a life completely externalized to the society and therefore not worthy of any support or enablement. What do people get upon prison release? A couple hundred dollars, and in any case, given recidivism rates, they are expected to be back sooner rather than later. Here's $200 for the coach fare home, see you in a few months. We'll fully pay your way back.

SSG: Yes, you've lost your right to food stamps, public housing, certain jobs ...

DTG: ... exactly. What other future is there for you but to return to the place from which we are just releasing you, the only home you have? There are occasional reports of former felons committing obvious petty crimes just to get shelter or food or medical treatment by being returned to prison. What kind of calculations are people forced into? And this is linked to the shift from the caretaker – the welfare – state, to the neoliberalizing traffic cop state. We all know the difficulties faced by the welfare state: the demise of the tax base that could fuel caretaking of any kind and the recourse in its wake to individualized forms of charity. So FEMA could not respond to Katrina or other natural disasters because it did not have the means. The prevailing forms of response become charitable, which then get streamed to ends of extended segregation identified by the principal people contributing to or directing the charities. Likewise, the responses to felons released, the services available to them, are overwhelmingly charitable services by those who have very few means at their disposal anyway. And all this has been done in a society that coterminously has defined itself by the slogan "No Child Left Behind."

Today we could probably revise that slogan to "All Non-Republican Voters Left Behind." In the 2012 national elections, Republicans lost the presidency, but the more radical wing of the party gained or extended their grip on state legislatures and governorships. They have become emboldened, most notably radically delimiting voting by those population segments unlikely to vote Republican combined with gerrymandering voting districts to ensure safe seats for radically conservative, overwhelmingly white candidates while lumping voters of color together in districts to delimit the broader political impact of their votes.

In North Carolina, like many other such states, Republicans have insisted on formal voter ID like a passport or driver's license less readily available to older, poorer, black and brown citizens. In the name of preventing voter fraud, for which no shred of evidence exists, legitimate voters are disenfranchised. In a remote rural county the controlling politicians have moved to deny voting rights to students at the historically black college Elizabeth City State University by considering them non-residential. Longstanding voting booth sites at or near the college have been closed down, requiring time-consuming, uncomfortable trips to whiter, more conservative parts of the county just to exercise one's right to vote. All this has been made possible by the US Supreme Court recently overturning that key provision of the 1965 Voting Rights Act requiring states with persistent histories of black voter repression to get prior clearance for any voting plan changes in the state. It is not that such state restrictions can no longer be challenged, but this is possible now only after they have been institutionalized and via long, expensive litigation. Other states are closely watching the constitutionality of North Carolina's efforts to see if they follow suit. As the US deigns to lecture the world about what it takes to make a polity democratic, forces systematically seek to deprive non-confirming and -conforming citizens of their right to exercise their vote. Democracy has become a mere shell in the name of which voting rights, the very heart of a democratic polity, are being obliterated, shellacked. It's obscene.

So you can see here the intricate interweaving of the carceral state, voting, and education. A more educated public tends to be less conservative, but also less criminalized. As the US becomes more demographically diverse, so, too, does its educated population. There is something else relatedly that happens in the second half of the 1980s. It starts under Reagan, becomes formalized under Bush I, and brings together a number of these forces in play. The attack on affirmative action had its gloves taken off in the early 1980s. William Bradford Reynolds, the Assistant Attorney General, was absolutely extreme in challenging affirmative action ...

SSG: ... who headed Reagan's civil rights office ...

DTG: ... that's right. Notice where the attack on affirmative action has been most visible. It's in those states with robust public university systems – Michigan,

New York, North Carolina, Florida, Texas, California, Washington State. It's down the East Coast, where you have black heterogeneity, across the South-West, where Latinos are concentrated, and up the West Coast, where Latinos and increasingly Asian Americans are constituting significant populations. So it's around the borders of the country. And it's also those places that into the early 1990s were suffering recession. We find here processes deeply related in their conditions of possibility. The insistence on a radically individualizing, privatizing, race-effacing sociality at its extreme produces unqualified homogeneity. It turns out that elite institutions of higher learning are attended overwhelmingly by the children of white parents; black and brown students largely attend "open access," much less effective, and often for-profit colleges that leave them professionally unprepared and deeply in debt.

There's an imperative to push back here, as on voting and incarceration, to see them as entangled, though we need to be thoughtful and not self-parodying when we do. Whites, predictably, insist on meritocratic criteria for college admission like grade point averages and standardized test scores so long as they privilege them in competition with black and brown students. When whites realize Asian Americans fare better than them on these measures, the same white respondents immediately prefer affirmative action considerations – for themselves [Jaschik 2013]! It is imperative to support dismissal with searingly critical arguments and counter-evidence. One needs to be able to show that the attack on college accessibility is also the economically and morally unsustainable insistence on incarcerability, both underpinned by the bald attempt at restricting voting rights. It's gated electioneering, not only gated communities. It's gated politics.

SSG: This recalls the astonishing remarks of former Secretary of Education William Bennett, "the hypocritical arbiter of America's moral values," as you rightly characterize him [2002a: 79], specifically the "thought experiment" he gave voice to on national radio. He was postulating that the abortion of all black infants would prove an effective means of nationwide crime reduction. A genocidal hypothesis ironically positing the heart of darkness, the barbaric slaughter of babies no less, at the very center of civil society, prompted in this case by neither indifference nor invisibility. This seems driven by a much older, "naturalistic" logic – in your terms – or perhaps something quite new, a neoliberally inspired revision of Social Darwinism, the "Survivor" mentality. How would you contextualize such abhorrent logic? Or for that matter the national public debate that ensued following Bennett's remarks, which queried whether they can properly be considered racist. (Shelby Steele appeared on CNN to defend Bennett against such allegations, citing the exorbitant overrepresentation of black men in US prisons.)

DTG: Both content and logic are utterly outrageous, the rhetorical reprise of the Tuskegee experiments. The genocidal suggestion signals a callousness, the contemporary heart of darkness. But even on its own logic, killing all black babies and therefore all future black people would not end crime. It might reduce crime to a degree to which that population now disproportionately criminalized would be wiped out. Given that whites commit crime, however, crime would still persist. Bennett's buddies seek to criminalize abortion, but remain silent if not Steele-like supportive when he calls for aborting all black babies. In any case, others would have to be targeted to fill the prisons because the political economy of prisons requires they be filled. Guards have to get paid. Write off prison workers too? That's a lot of blood, metaphorically and literally, on Mr Moral Majority's hands. It is worth noting that Bennett was also national drug czar under Bush I, a key rationalizer in the criminalization of black drug use.

Bennett's self-authorization to speak publicly in this way signals a deeper social re-authorization by whites to express deadly terms about black and brown people. Reagan made it increasingly easy again after the 1960s to raise issues around race that had been rendered not just uncivil but de-authorized. Recall the Willie Horton ad. Reagan was cashing in on the success of Nixon's Southern strategy. Racial issues again became the medium for articulating the politics of white *ressentiment*. Obama's election was taken as license to open the floodgates. A recent Stanford study reveals that just over half of Americans admit to racial bias, notably against blacks and Latinos. Implicit racial bias is up 7 percentage points to 56 percent. Among the loudest facilitators: Ann Coulter, Joe Walsh, Rush Limbaugh, Fox news commentators, Tea Partiers, the endless slew of racist internet images of the Obamas.

You can read all of this in sum as materializations of the Racial Privacy Act, as realizing the extensions of racisms privatized without the social apparatus to address it, as racisms' proliferations in the absence not just of race but of any social capacity to recognize them as expressions of racism. It is not just that racisms produce social death, in their limit cases; it is that the conditions of their recognition and identification have been buried, alive, too. We are, it could be said, conceptually and socially screwed.

9
Racial (ir)relevance

SSG: There has emerged recently a deep tension between claims that racism is over and the insistence that not only is it not over but it has intensified of late. How do you read this widening gulf?

DTG: It's obvious to anyone who cares to look that there have been widespread racial renewals and proliferating expressions of racisms, often in denial of both the racial register and any racist intent. Against this background it must be asked what the claims to postraciality, to racial irrelevance, amount to. The recourse to a discourse of postraciality must be understood first in the context of the long history of nonracisms. I put this in the plural, because the histories both of racisms, as I have been stressing throughout, and of nonracialisms and antiracisms have never been singular.

If racisms have always signaled divided, excluded, segregated, and unequal socialities, the nonracial at times has referenced the ideal of a common, shared humanity. That there is no race but the human race, emphasized after World War II, especially captures this sense. In the nineteenth century, nonracialism in concept, even if the term was not yet actually in use, conjured the reach for abolition, an imagination of emancipated life where race would be shed as if society's outer skin. After the civil rights movement and helping to animate anti-apartheid, the nonracial stood for the erasure of difference and social division predicated on race, but also for the reach for equalizing sameness as the baseline for addressing issues of social justice, issues of the basic equality and dignity of the person embedded in conceptions of universal moral and human rights. Drawing on these legacies, perhaps even presuming and trading on their success, post-raciality has been invoked to signal "the end of racism," and no doubt more cynically also of the redressive programs and measures advanced or adopted to address the debilitating legacies of racial injustice, from slavery to segregation.

SSG: You've distinguished in your work between "color-blind racism," "antiracialism," and, even more provocatively, "born again racism." The latter has clear religious connotations. The "born again" seems implicitly to invoke renewed racial configurations such as Muslims, G.W. Bush's war on terror as crusade, and the clash of civilizations, pitting white Christians against newly raced Muslims. But such a formulation might also invoke the racially significant history of evangelism in US slave and post-slave societies. And the millennium evokes the kind of millenarian significance as centuries and millennia end and commence. Your explicit context here is South African racial politics, though it clearly resonates with a centuries-old puritan vision of the shining city on the hill or the Rapture.

DTG: Racial commitments are always about convictions, or their intensification. The content of the convictions shifts over time, the intensity modulated or multiplied in different social contexts. The messianic quality is always there, at least implicitly, as the idea of a utopian end state to be strived after as well as being held at bay in order to extend the striving, which becomes the very point. Arrival disappoints, never lives up to the advance billing. It is the striving – in racial terms to produce the purity of the social, to purge the bruising populations, to expunge the enemy – that is the object of investment, the extension and intensification of conviction. The expulsion of the Moors from Spain in 1492 hardly ended the presence of Muslims in Europe. The point was never completely to end the Muslim presence, for that ending would rob Europe of a contrast by which it has always defined itself. Whether the presence is actual or projected, virtual, it always is accompanied by the imaginary. The "nonracial" – here, the not-racial state – similarly involves a striving. Both extend the endless waiting, preparing oneself in the striving for the end state, the endgame, to manifest. Today, the striving has become existentially, if not commercially, cheap. Perhaps the very point is to turn the struggle – itself signaling effort – into a purchase, the shift from existential to the cost of merely commercial investment. Buy the t-shirt, donate to charity or the demeaning website, retweet the insulting cartoons or comments. But don't go out on the street with others to make a movement.

Colorblind racism is an elaboration in the context of the US, an expression articulated in different ways in other places under the rubric of nonracialism ...

SSG: ... or racelessness ...

DTG: ... right, so the kind of business-promoted non-racialism we find in South Africa, from the 1960s onwards, in multiculturalism in Canada or Australia, or in parts of Europe. Those forms of racelessness or purging race and everything race has stood for tend to unmark the expressed racism as a consequence. Anti-*racialism* is the process that produces this narrowed sense of nonracialism.

SSG: Yes, I had imagined it to be much more activist, intervening, interventionist, where colorblindness seems to mark a sensibility.

DTG: Colorblindness is supposed to be the outcome where we live by some version of "don't judge me by the color of my skin but by the content of my character" – that now revealing cliché which gets so flippantly invoked. Colorblindness is the "don't ask, don't tell" of racial politics. It is the politics of the sociality of the skin by other means, avoidability rather than engagement.

In *The Ground Beneath Her Feet* [2000], Salman Rushdie's self-indulgent novel about the history of rock 'n' roll, there is this one beautiful line about "life at the frontier of the skin." This is a fabulously suggestive phrase, calling for elaboration. How easy it is to characterize someone as white or black, describing to a person you have never met whom they will be waiting

173

for, what look to expect in order to find each other. The frontier of the skin becomes a default reference.

What sociality does skin carry with it? What social landscape sits behind that frontier, what does it leave behind and presuppose? What do people *see* when they first see each other, when, as Tom Mitchell [2012] puts it, they see *through* race? Lewis Gordon has written on the phenomenology of racial experience in and through the skin, in a Fanonian sense. What one sees, what one doesn't, what brings pleasure, or displeasure, anger, fear, or anxiety. This broadened notion of the sociality of the skin becomes a reference point. But this sociality – the presuppositions, investments, historical arrangements, structural orderings – is also instantaneously denied. And it is the denial that goes under the rubric of "antiracialism." It doesn't go away, it gets repressed, pushed under, it gets almost pushed underwater – I'll use a New Orleans metaphor here, to think about what antiracialism does. Likewise with racelessness, with colorblindness as socio-psychological condition; these, too, are socialities of the skin because they take their reference points from the racial even in denial. Explicitly in denial, to press the point. Buried, but alive. In that buried but living condition, what traces are left, ruts in the road that one staggers over, and what emerges in what I have called "born again racism"?

SSG: Can you spell out a bit what you have intended by "born again racism"?

DTG: Born again racism is racism of the habits of the heart. There is no longer a sociality of race taken to undergird the racial as an explicit reference point. Where racist expression is so much as acknowledged, it is admitted only as the expression of the bad apple "we" can send to re-education camp to make everything okay. This is the racism of history's erasure, of histories, about which we spoke earlier. It's racism rendered invisible. And these obscurings and opacities are linked to neo-liberal individualization. This is of our present time precisely because neo-individualizing has been elevated to being the only point of reference, the singular foundation of social ontology. Collectivity becomes rhetorically, socially unacceptable, and collective action is turned into the anomaly. The lack of a sustained social movement about any deep, abiding concern – about war, about racism, about spiraling inequalities, about surveillance and the death of privacy, about state repression, secrecy, and incarceration – has deeply to do with this neo-individualizing condition that removes the collective as one's point of reference and requires one to fall back on one's own devices, to act only as an individual. Flash mobs are not social movements. In the end, you are an individual looking after your own interests and have to fend for yourself. The structural conditions of possibility have disappeared as an acknowledged defining condition of social positioning.

SSG: Born again evokes a kind of fundamentalism as it gets mapped now. It is a conferral of agency on some other site and complete repudiation of responsibility except for individual responsibility. It's just you and your personal savior.

DTG: Precisely. Which seems so much of our time. It is the *new* New Age. Though I'm characterizing this in terms of "the born again," this is not to say that it ever died. It just morphed ...

SSG: ... rejuvenated ...

DTG: ... got resurrected. Racial expression now proliferates, absent the explicit invocation of the category of race. Racist expression, structurally as much as individually, pulses under the guise of its constant disavowal and denial.

Almost wherever one cares to look, one can find evidence of renewed racisms. A survey in 2011 revealed that a little more than a fifth of Mississippi adults think racial intermarriage wrong (nearly half of Republicans) and almost 30 percent are unsure (over 10 percent of Republicans – perhaps a mark of Republicans today, they are sure even, maybe especially, when wrong). So half the adults in the state think there is something at least questionable about miscegenation. These numbers are comparable to those around *Loving v. Virginia* (the 1968 Supreme Court case rendering unconstitutional any outlawing of interracial marriage).

The two great black models of the 1980s, Bethann Hardison and Iman, both now turned fashion industry activists, have been evidencing how non-diverse, and especially how unfriendly to black models, the fashion industry and the runway remain [see Wilson 2013]. Significantly fewer black and brown models are being used today for the shows of major couture houses than in the 1980s, reinforcing the sense that the standards of aesthetic beauty are still represented by whiteness and defined by a power establishment remaining overwhelmingly white. Black workers continue to suffer unemployment in the US at twice the rate of whites, and income and wealth inequality between whites and blacks has actually grown significantly wider in the past decade, not least as affirmative action in college admissions has come under withering attack from conservatives.

The President of Hillsdale College, a small Michigan school, recently bemoaned state bureaucrats visiting his college to look for "dark ones" on campus [see Klein 2013]. (He was complaining to legislators about the state's interest in "enforcing" diversity on campus.) The college issued an apology for any "offense taken," effectively abrogating personal culpability, while insisting that President Arnn's concern was to point out "the state-endorsed racism." Remember, this is Michigan, a Northern state, in 2013, not George Wallace's Alabama in 1963, though a state where affirmative action has been hotly contested.

To give this a more global ring, speaking on the BBC about the fiery London responses to the Mark Duggan killing by police in 2011, historian David Starkey characterized the visibly white riotous looters as having "become black," as though urban violence and looting are naturalistically characteristic of black culture, but anomalies among whites. By contrast, Brazil is often held up as racially advanced because of both its large and celebrated racially mixed demography and, since Lula's Presidency, its emphatic state support for affirmative action for the racial poor. And yet in the private sphere things are not quite so ideal. Anitta is an emerging pop star who has brought favela funk into mainstream Brazilian and world pop. As the national and global spotlights have fallen on her, her record label, Warner Bros in Brazil, has insisted on whitening her image, scrubbing her skin (it is unclear whether literally with skin bleach, with cosmetics, or via photoshopped images), trading blackness for a more sensational but also stereotypical stardom [see Watts 2013].

SSG: Given all of this – and you could go on almost endlessly with cases like this today – what do you make of the claim to postraciality?

DTG: We must ask what exactly, in the face of all this counter-evidence, the claim to postraciality amounts to. Far from the final demise of racism, postraciality is the new register in which racial commitments today are expressed. Postraciality is racisms' contemporary modality of expression. It is the register of nonracial racisms, those racisms not just without race but in the absence, the erasure of the possibility even of identifying racism and the injustices for which it has always been taken to stand. Postraciality is to the history of racisms what postcoloniality is to the colonial. It is not so much a break as an extension, not the end but a new expressive beginning, not the demise but the revived, the resurrected, the "born again," offering a new lease on life.

Trayvon Martin's tragically premature death manifests – and so exemplifies – the sociologics and socialities of postraciality. Postraciality is a sociality of the skin rendered less literal, more metaphorical. George Zimmerman, the neighborhood vigilante; Trayvon Martin, the stalked teenager minding his own business. The adult vigilante carries a gun; the teenager nothing but candy and a cold drink. Zimmerman presumes, stereotypes, calls police, pursues even when warned by the dispatcher to let alone; Trayvon minds his own business, becomes concerned, calls a girlfriend, confronts ... his stalker. Trayvon is walking while black; Zimmerman is suspicious while driving. Trayvon has had some school disciplinary issues but, with obviously strong, supportive, caring parents, no police run-ins; Zimmerman has a history of accusations against him of felonious assault and domestic violence, and at least one criminal charge which his father, a retired Florida judge, helped quash. The boy walking is called "a punk" by the man driving, because dressed like "a thug" (which Bill O'Reilly reiterated as the explanation, if not justification, for Martin's killing). The racially profiled boy pursued is expected to give way; the adult pursuer is given every right to stand his ground. Sound historically familiar? The young suspect is dead, the accuser the accused; the accused is legally exonerated, guiltless in the eyes of the law. The accused's confidant and lead spokesman in the immediate wake of the killing appeared repeatedly on a white supremacist podcast arguing for racial segregation while mouthing off racist comments [see Blake 2013]. And race apparently has no place in the case?

How, then, does postraciality operate racially? There are a series of racial operators driving the raciologics of postraciality. First, *racial reversibility*. Victims become victimizers, victimizers victims. Zimmerman the stalker becomes Zimmerman the stalked; Martin the stalked becomes the aggressor. A recent Rasmussen poll ...

SSG: ... that polling outfit that got the last presidential election so wrong in favor of Romney?

DTG: Yeah, them. Their poll [Rasmussen 2013] found that more Americans – double actually – find blacks to be more racist than whites or Hispanics. The numbers are significantly higher for Republicans. No indication is offered for the grounds on which the charges would be based. But one can imagine: that blacks take whites to be arrogant, powerful, or discriminatory; that blacks find whites to be privileged, offensive, abusive. The charge is both reversed and the reversal is predicated on a relative trivialization of what racism amounts to, the "evidence" imagined or anecdotal rather than for the most part directly experienced.

Mark O'Mara, Zimmerman's lead lawyer, insinuated racial reversibility in claiming after his trial that had Zimmerman been black he would not have been charged at all. Today, apparently, blacks control the processes of criminalization, whites increasingly nothing. News, I am sure, to most black Americans, and flying in the face of all the counter-evidence (recall "stop and frisk"). Surely it is more realistic to conclude that had Zimmerman been black it is far more likely he would not have stalked a teenager minding his own business on his way home from the convenience store. Similarly, Dan Riehl, a conservative US blogger, tweeted in the wake of Obama's comments about the Trayvon Martin case that "Obama is the first Racist in Chief."

In the primary election to replace Michael Bloomberg as New York City's mayor, the leading Democratic candidate, Bill de Blasio, criticized Bloomberg's twelve-year mayoralty as favoring the rich at the poor's expense. A political progressive, de Blasio is married to a black woman, their two children mixed, the son sporting the largest Afro "since Angela Davis," as one commentator put it. Bloomberg publicly chided de Blasio for "running a racist campaign" because he had featured a photograph of his mixed-race family in a campaign commercial [see McGeehan 2013]. For Bloomberg, the use of the photograph was a not-so-veiled attempt to curry support from the considerable African-American population in New York City. The infamous Willie Horton ad in reversible redux.

For O'Mara and Bloomberg, postraciality presupposes the end of racial terms. Given that "the fact of blackness," blacks' very being and presence, as Fanon [1956] characterized it, is of necessity racial, their existence, presence, and practice, on this casuistry, must be racist. Postraciality's cheap logic; raciality's easy extension in the name of racial erasure. This erasure is made all the easier by postraciality's denial of historical relevance, the ongoing impact of history's contemporary legacy. "We are not responsible for the long-gone slavery, Jim Crow, or segregation of our forebears," postraciality's *dehistoricizing* refrain usually goes. Well, maybe, but segregation, less cohesive and informally produced and sustained, nevertheless remains today. So how about that?

Second, when a person today is accused of or outed for racist expression, the default response is to claim *no intentionality*. No racial thought crossed the mind. Zimmerman had no racist intention so couldn't have been racist. Absent intention, Zimmerman had – really could have – no agency in the Event. The agency was all Trayvon Martin's. He supposedly struck first, pummeled and pressed down on a motionless Zimmerman. Trayvon the aggressor, Zimmerman the aggrieved; Trayvon the violent, Zimmerman the passive; Trayvon the agent, Zimmerman the acted upon. The black man-child, lacking reason, ironically becomes agent; the white adult, supposedly a rational person, is devoid of reason and so no agent.

Third, postraciality insists that "racism is over, so stop talking about it." Elspeth Reeve [2012], a journalist for *The Atlantic*, has articulated this most literally in writing that "Racism is dead, the only people who think it still exists are liberals." She of course has not bothered to attend to "born again racism." Hans von Spakovsky, who heads up the Election Law Reform Initiative for the ultra-conservative Heritage Foundation and who has vigorously defended Republican efforts to delimit the capacity to vote, tweeted that "race had nothing to do with what happened in Sanford [the George Zimmerman killing of Trayvon Martin] & that we have less racism today than at any point in our history." Having erased race, antiracialists are now trying to rub out a lexicon by which to keep racism visible and indeed risible. We are being led more and more into a terrain of racisms without racism, of the phenomena without the analytic terms by which to reference or even recognize let alone critically address the condition(s).

President Obama is deemed the register both that we are in the time of postraciality and not there yet, the former by the mere fact that a black man has been elected US President, the latter that he sometimes still references America's abiding racial conditions. He is the register of postraciality more deeply because read by those fearful of losing racially authorized power with the ascension of more black politicians to state and city power, to having direct access to, if not heightened control of, the levers of state and urban direction. The only times President Obama has violated his carefulness about (not) speaking about race have been about the uncontested police harassment, even profiling, of a black person of his class position (the Skip Gates case) and the racial profiling by a neighborhood vigilante of a young black man, a boy still, who could have been Obama's son or Obama himself at a younger age. Stop and frisk, and vigilante violence.

As the insistence intensifies that racism is dead and we should stop talking about it, the rationalizers of racelessness quickly insinuate racial reference into their characterizations of events on which they are commenting, trading as always on the sociality of the skin to advance self-interest. Conservative commentators paradoxically refer to the President invariably as black, insist that Trayvon Martin would not be dead but for his thug clothing, attitude, and self-presentation (read racial characterizations). As racial profiling proliferates, even when rendered unconstitutional by the Supreme Court, raceless rationalizations ratchet up.

SSG: How to think about Muslims within this framework?

DTG: Muslims are the perfect postracial subjects. Neither black nor Latino, perceived as the anti-Jew, their raciality is ambiguous. The US Supreme Court has a long history of troubling over the exact racial status of various Middle Easterners – white, not white, black, even Indian-like? Their ambiguous status makes it more difficult to dismiss as racist demeaning, discriminatory, and dismissive expressions against Muslims. Longstanding presumptions of *non*-belonging, reinforced by racially resonant animus, mark Muslims as racially transparent. Their racial transparency – a religious identification, after all – makes them racially unrecognizable and, para-doxically, racially fixed, fixatedly racial. Extended meanings to racial religiosity, religious raciality.

Too often a racially driven culture of suspicion, belligerence, and aggression by those who (take themselves to) represent forces of authority leads to death, the death of those taken not to belong, considered to be up to no good, socially unproductive. That, too, is part of the structural conditions producing the death of an innocent black 17-year-old walking home minding his own business but also of Sikhs mistaken for Muslims in the wake of 9/11, the deadly shooting up of a Sikh gurdwara in Wisconsin, the burning of the Qur'an by Terry Jones in Florida or by US soldiers in Afghanistan and charges of urinating on the Qur'an made in Guantánamo, or the ugly public reaction to the selection of the first Indian American woman as Miss America 2013, because "dark, Muslim, Arab, terrorist, unAmerican" (all terms used in the blogosphere to character-assassinate her – I'll refrain from comments about the pageant).

This, then, is the legacy, the raciologics of postraciality. Race is irrelevant, it has no social matter. But race matters, where relevant, where it orders the social and extends socialities of the skin, with all their preferences enabled, privileges extended, and possibilities effectively eventuated. So here we have the unstated slogan of postracial sociality: "*Race* is dead. Long live *racisms* (without race, without racism)."

10

Reiteracing Obama

SSG: The election in 2008 of Barack Obama and his re-election in 2012 as US President have been perceived by critics and pundits alike as a culminating triumph of decades-long civil rights struggles for racial equality but also their final nail in the coffin. The elections may serve to absolve white liberal guilt and may put paid to qualms about the nation's egregious racial history despite the continued impacts of that historical legacy on the vast majority of people of color. Given your critique of the contemporary colorblind insistence that "race no longer matters," that the nation largely refuses to engage with, even see, ongoing racist inequality and exclusion, how does Obama's victory perpetuate, or complicate, the presumption of a postracial America?

DTG: Barack Obama embodies the racial tensions of American and global postraciality: We are beyond race but fixed and fixated by it. This is self-evident nationally: the license to say anything racist, including charges of racial reversibility and denial of racism, followed by a quick condemnation, denial, dissembling. And globally the sense that if America has twice elected a black president, the world largely has gotten over its long modern history of racism. If globally racism always expressed itself elsewhere, the "over there," and that over there was invariably the US or South Africa, the fact that both apparently have marched on means that we, "here," no longer have to concern ourselves with race too. There may be issues with immigration, with diversity, with multiculturalism, but these apparently have no defining racial dimension. Or so postraciality would have it.

The political phenomenon of Obama – Obamania – represents a range of continuities and shifts in American racial life, and in raciality more generally. As many have pointed out, there has been a claim by those who either want to "get beyond race" or no longer think race is relevant to say that this is the crowning achievement of the civil rights logic and legacy and that America has now largely, if not completely, closed the chapter on its sordid racial and racist history. There is a whole range of counter-evidence to suggest that this is far too optimistic a view. Since at least Reconstruction, black unemployment rates have doubled those of whites, as true today as 125 years ago. Latino unemployment rates are lower than blacks' but significantly higher than those for whites, even after disaggregating for education, age, and so on. So the claim that Obama's elections are symptomatic of a closure is too hasty.

Second, it's obviously an important development that a man who is African American, of mixed-race descent, who represents a whole range of heterogeneities, of a decidedly middle-class family background and who was

educated at some of the most notable educational institutions in the US, is able to rise to the most powerful
position in the country, if not the world. He gets re-
elected with a very considerable proportion of white
and other non-African-American, especially Latino,
voters in this country. So Obama has permanently shuf-
fled America's electoral map.

His election very quickly gave way to all kinds of
push-backs, a good deal of them racially inflected. This
is another indication that the sense of race has shifted,
but not completely altered or disappeared. Rather, it has
dis-appeared, reappearing elsewhere, transforming into
other modalities of racial and racist expression.

The third point ties to the first, speaking directly to
questions of avoiding issues of inequality. Inequality in
America has not just persisted since emancipation; it has
dramatically deepened since the Reagan administration,
especially in the last decade, exacerbated by Bush–
Cheney policies. Today, the top 1 percent of the wealthy
own approximately 35 percent of the wealth, the top
20 percent own 80 percent, and the bottom 20 percent
just 1 percent. The 400 wealthiest Americans command
as much wealth as the bottom half of the population
(more than 155 *million* people). This has further skewed
political and social power in favor of the massively
wealthy, who tend to be overwhelmingly white.

Obama has done little to roll back such inequality.
He has sought to regulate wealth generation a bit more
closely, to rein in some of the extremes, but he has
largely been timid in the face of dominant interests.
Arguably, what the Obama administration has stood
for makes it much more difficult to address the racial
components of these inequalities. Derrick Bell [1992]

contended repeatedly that in the US the only way, politically, to address racial inequality was through universal
programs addressing inequality generally, from which
some black folk, at least, would benefit, a version of
trickle-down political economy. The trouble is that the
Obama administration has made scant attempts to
address even general levels of inequality, other than
health care concerns, little to push directly for quality
job growth for the poor and middle classes while his
policies have made Wall Street investors far wealthier.
And he has been fairly tepid about defending against
attacks on affirmative action, for example.

SSG: Many Obama critics argue that despite his centrist
rhetoric, his politics are neoliberal. In what ways is
this the case, or does he represent what you call neo-
neoliberalism, its hyper condition? This seems particularly relevant to his handling of the financial crisis,
especially given its impact on the racial poor. Can you
comment on this?

DTG: Aspects of his politics are both neoliberal and the
hyper condition I'm calling neo-neoliberal, the tighten-
ing of the screws, the ratcheting up of conditions that
constitute the neoliberal itself. In many instances,
Obama's politics and the extension of the policies he
inherited reproduce neoliberal commitments, and in
some more extreme instances neo-neoliberal ones. His,
you could say, is a neoliberalism with a human face. (I
hesitate to admit neo-neoliberalism can have a human
face, as the Tea Party-led government shutdown in
October 2013 made self-evident.)

Now in Obama's unstinting focus on stabilizing the country's financial system, the one massive failure of economic, let alone political, imagination by the administration was to pay no initial attention to joblessness. Little thought was given to rewarding potential employers directly for hiring people they otherwise would not, and not just bailing out large corporations. That inattention to working possibilities was also a racial inattention. As un- and radical underemployment ballooned, and as housing values dropped precipitously, most Americans spiraled downward into red ink. One could almost say that this debt deepening across wide swaths of the public was also a symbolic "blackening" of America, the spiraling sense for increasing proportions of what the economic experience has long been for most black people in America. It was the proliferation across the population of living in a critical condition. This failure of imagination speaks to the burgeoning hold of neoliberal logic on US economic policy makers.

SSG: But there was also the failure of any kind of critical inquiry that would have a transformative impact. When you think of the two major bubbles, housing and the toxic mortgages that devastated especially black communities, and the other one that has become more recently evident around for-profit universities, they have disproportionately affected homeless, poor, and work-challenged people desiring to improve their prospects by going to school. These have deep racial impacts too.

DTG: Educational opportunity has been crucial, but the debt burden many students now have to assume for that access is exploitative rather than enabling. The prospective employability with the certification they acquire from the for-profits mostly is an illusion, at best. And it is students of color who have been most impacted. Congressional and presidential inability to delimit this exploitation exacerbates the hyper-neglect long haunting the working and now increasingly workless and racial poor.

Neoliberalization involves intense privatization, the reshaping of what is possible, of regulatory regimes, adding new kinds of instruments of control, including radical job loss. Neoliberalism, in short, is the intensification of social regulation to protect the deregulation of the economic. It emphasizes commercial enterprise, personal entrepreneurship, and the genius of individual innovation as the economic driving force – what I earlier called "participatory individualism" – while delimiting all conception and support of public good(s) and social care. (Consider the virulent attack on Obamacare by Republicans with no alternative than to cast adrift people who cannot afford care.) Participatory individualism restricts social participation to individual preference and choice, reducing racist expression to individual "outbreaks" that might go viral as other individuals take it up, as Chandiren Valayden [2013] has put it, but which expression by private individuals remains both beyond the purview of and so protected by the state.

We are living in increasingly critical conditions – climatically, economically, and indeed politically. The social fabric is fragile. The question becomes how to mobilize a critical response adequate to addressing these critical conditions, to counter the spiral of pervasive financialization, deepening debt, the culture of radical individualization of risk, the politics of participatory individualism, historical amnesia, and the sociality of protecting privatized racisms in the name of racial reversibilities (or charging with racism those most targeted by its expressions).

SSG: This anticipates my follow-up. One might rephrase the problem in starker terms. Obama has been careful to distance himself from a prior civil rights generation, never claiming to be their spokesperson, or advocate, least of all their avenger. His self-presentation is rather that of a "mixed" person, a "mongrel," or, in his terms a "mutt" – a characterization purposively "postracial" or "post-ethnic," even "post-essentialist." As an individual, he's transcended the ascribed collective, categorical inferiority (whether biologically or culturally inscribed) against which his predecessors have struggled for centuries. Yet, it's not at all clear that this victory has invalidated the underlying presumption of this claimed inferiority. In fact, such logic arguably has become more entrenched: If some individuals have risen above alleged "collective defects," the failure of the vast majority is the result of their moral degeneracy, lack of work ethic, or inherent incapacity, as the claim goes. If Obama is the face of "the new America," isn't the experience of most people of color captured in what you call "racial duress," a condition of permanent humiliation and perpetual violence?

DTG: Clearly, the bifurcation of conditions that your question presupposes runs very deep in the US. Obama is the moderate and moderating but still representative *neoliberal* subject. This is evidenced in his stressing personal responsibility over structural conditions, in exerting a muscularity regarding policing, warring, securitization, and surveillance even as he parades that muscularity as moderate, middle-of-the-roadish, commonsensical. In a sense he humanizes these positions, his personal likeability almost making it harder to criticize the objectionable elements of the policies and their actualization. The NSA and drone actions are the most disturbing in this regard, not to mention repatriation of undocumented migrants and extradition.

There has been a shift in the racial characterization of the desperate in the US increasingly from blacks to those presumed outsiders, Latinos and Muslims. Blacks in the cultural rhetoric of the loose-tongued right are less a threat than a nuisance, the perennial problem, moochers and takers. Mexicans are presumptuously illegal, Muslims stereotypically terrorists. So, the conditions are slightly different for different demographic elements. Also, one doesn't want to overlook the incredibly and increasingly stressful conditions faced by the white unemployed and working class, those who had hitherto taken themselves to be a step into the middle class and no longer are, who have lost homes and employment, and increasingly are facing the loss of welfare support and now food stamps. Food stamps average $1.40 support per meal for the indigent, overwhelmingly but not only people of color, while Members of Congress who are cutting food support for these folks receive a daily food allowance of $127. The neoliberal commandment to "help yourself" takes on newly ambiguous significance in this context.

Obama complexly, sometimes contradictorily, embodies this confluence of concerns. There is his celebrated capacity to get beyond race, while invisibility of the racial to which he often silently aspires ratchets up under conditions of postraciality. The postracial extends the presence of the racial, masquerading behind its invisibility. This invisibility paradoxically also exhibits visible expression, in the sense that raciality is visible to one even as one might misrecognize or refuse to recognize its presence. And you could take Obama's own racial characterization as symptomatic of that very confluence – it's obviously visible to us, and at the same time invisible, because he looks like any corporate head, his race sometimes almost disappearing. We are reminded to forget his raciality at certain moments, only to be jarred back into it by Tea Party characterizations or other forms of implicit or explicit reference, even occasionally by his mimicking the loping gait of street blackness [see Wing 2013]. One has to note, though, that these recognitions and misrecognitions, the racial visibility or invisibility to others, are rarely remotely under the control of the raced subject. In that sense, Obama represents, and he is symptomatic of, exactly the condition of race in the late modern moment: both the visibility of his raciality and the invisibility of it represent the invisibility of the duress that racial characterization so often carries with it, and its invisibility to the rest of America.

SSG: You could almost say the same thing about the oral, given his lack of marked speech that so many politicians have pointed out ...

DTG: Yes, exactly. The remarks of Senate Majority Leader Harry Reid about Obama's speech – that he spoke "with no Negro dialect, unless he wanted to have one" – bore this out. The President's speech is to America what the King's speech was to Britain …

SSG: … but the silence of that duress as well … He is President, to be sure, but even as such he's deeply reticent to exercise his "free speech" on matters racial, even less inclined to expression in the black vernacular.

DTG: Obama can talk street, even if he rarely if ever does publicly. Having grown up all over the world, largely with white grandparents and mother, mostly outside of an African-American community, he *became* African American rather than being born one or born into that community. His street inflection came late, with college and community organizing, and could be characterized as a form of mimicry, were he to and where he does adopt it. His natural form of expression is not especially recognizable as African American, whatever stereotypically might be meant by this; it is almost neutralized. If you didn't know his voice, and heard him on the radio, he would be one of those voices, you know, … is he or isn't he? Vocality is not unimportant, not unlike the visibility of his condition. It is neutralized, I don't want to say quite muted, through the well-tailored suits, the impeccable dress, the bearing. Perhaps he is most African American on the basketball court, not to over-characterize it, precisely because the basketball court is so racially indexed. He plays almost every day, it's his form of exercise and release, much as others might run, swim, hike, bike, or whatever. Much as Bush Jr. biked, Obama plays basketball, the one an isolated individualized activity, the other a team, social activity.

It's to these cultural moments of racial identification that those who want to pin Obama down racially might turn. Curiously, that stereotype is not played up in the Tea Party rhetoric. For "birthers" it couldn't be because it would immediately accept him as American, if begrudgingly, in his African-Americanity. His *African*-ity is played up in the Tea Party rhetoric, in contrast to his African-*American*-ity, the performativity of a past that also is not really his, as he readily points out.

SSG: Let's back up around the question of relative mutedness. The question of voice or silencing is even clearer when we consider the degree of success with which Obama, now leader of the free world, has been not so freely able to engage with (or disengage from) racially charged issues of the day – from his criticism of the Cambridge police for arresting Harvard Professor Henry Louis Gates in his own house, a charge that ended in apologetic backpedaling, even a White House "beer summit," to the Trayvon Martin case, about which we have spoken, and the unchecked nature of more systemic forms of racially prompted exclusion: black unemployment; the skyrocketing rates of incarceration for people of color; inflamed anti-immigration sentiment increasingly translated into public policy in states like Arizona; and viral Muslimania around inflammatory issues every so often. How do you account for this apparent reticence, or inability?

DTG: Obama's position is impossible. The first person of black background to assume the office of the Presidency, a person who, in his campaigning and somewhat in his governing, has sought, in his own terms, to transcend, to rise above, the politics of the racial. In that sense he *aspires* to postraciality of a sort. But that aspiration, as we've seen again and again, and as he himself must have experienced repeatedly, is an impossibility. He's brought down to earth very fast. He enters for the first time as the resident of a White House in which black people previously have worked and lived only as servants and service labor, as made clear by Clarence Lusane's terrific [2010] history *The Black History of the White House* (which I was privileged to read in manuscript form) and the recent movie *The Butler*.

SSG: I wonder how you assess Obama's quickly backing off his comment about policing, given its thoroughgoing, ongoing history in American life. A lot of African Americans were rather upset – elated first that it was recognized, made a comment of, and then feeling a bit abandoned?

DTG: There have been repeated moments of that sense of abandonment. That backtracking was one very visible indication of it. Whatever actually happened, Henry Louis Gates probably reacted in a huff, as perhaps anybody having one's home invaded by a policeman understandably would. The episode was characteristic of American policing generally and maybe the kind of violence of intervention on the part of the US state – the NSA again is the most revealing example – both internally and externally, in terms of its sense of securitization. When you contrast policing in some other countries (the Netherlands comes to mind), there was no need to arrest and handcuff a person for perhaps saying something nasty, an epithet, getting vocally angry in one's own home, but not physically violent. Policing in America is notable for its excessiveness, its impatience, not least racially prompted. The policing excessiveness and impatience were uncalled for.

American policing tends to profiling violence, especially in relation to African Americans. Obama's even tepid recognition of the raw nerve was not unimportant. He recognized it for the country as an overstepping of boundaries, an unreasonable response, and spoke to the experience of almost every African-American person, every person of color, in the country at some point in their lives; it is to his credit that he chose to address this. He was much maligned by conservatives for jumping to conclusions [see Bouie 2013]. The politics of the moment – and this is not to exonerate him for stepping back and losing his courage – exerts intense pressure, which gets brought to bear when people don't like what a politician, in this case the President, says.

Race again factors into this. Having taken himself to be above race, Obama now was clearly in the midst of it, feeling terribly uncomfortable and, as he put it nicely, backtracked as quickly as possible. And in doing so it became a "Kumbaya" moment, a facile racial reconciliation, a boys' "beer summit." It was a laughable moment rather than the more elevated "teachable" moment, to use Obama's own terms, it could have, and probably should have, become about the condition of wrongful conviction, or wrongful suspicion. There's a clear line, a *chain* that goes between wrongful suspicion and wrongful conviction in American criminal justice. The wrongful conviction of people of color – their over-indictment and over-prosecution – begins at the point of suspicion. It's at that point that black and brown people are brought into the structures of the criminal justice system, at which point the logic has already taken over. Today one in three adult black men in the US will be imprisoned in their life, one in six Latinos, and one in seventeen white men [see Knafo 2013]. This could have been a really important teachable moment about that chain of conditions – and I use that term "chain" pointedly – from the moment of wrongful suspicion (trying to unlock one's own door as suspicion of breaking into somebody else's house) and almost inevitable conviction. Obama lost his courage, he lost his mojo, at that point, and stepped back from using the presidential bully pulpit to make an important racial point. That's unfortunate.

Now postraciality, we're reminded, always bears its raciality with it. So the postracial is both post- and racial, and it's in that combination that Obama finds himself stuck, even as he seeks to transcend it time after time. The time after is always also a time within, is always a voice that speaks neutrally, but is made additionally to represent that which it's perceived to be. So, both its visibility and its vocality are always merged together into this reminder that the postracial is inevitably re-racially configured. This aspiration to get beyond bumps up against the racial realities on the ground of American life. Obama would have to be, literally, completely silent and almost thoroughly invisible to sustain the image, the affect, the illusion if not delusion, of being absolutely not racial – I don't say nonracial, but not racial. In America as much today as in the past, it's an impossibility, especially for someone in that position. He bears that burden, and here he's carried himself remarkably. It is the burden not just of a *first*

– breaking the color bar of the Presidency – but also the burden of carrying himself in that role, and constantly reminding us, even without saying it, that America is, *remains*, deeply racially configured, and that whatever is done in the figure of and around race – which is pretty much everything – is a burden and a cost for everybody to bear, and he's the one who symbolically bears it most.

Perhaps what has been most revealing about Obama's Presidency has less to do with the particular characteristics of this man who became President – the great man/ failed man histories of the Presidency – than with what it tells us about the constitutively racial ordering of the presidential office itself. This or that president can move things a little this way or that. But structurally the office represents the state's self-making, its history and legacy of social ordering. In the US these are deeply racially constituted. American sociality is renewed repeatedly in racially ordered and ordering terms. Self-election is also an insistence on self-selection, on who belongs and who does not, on presumptions of who is, can be, ought to be, properly American. Self-selection is inherently exclusionary, shedding from the body (politic) those taken inherently not to count, to belong. Obama's Presidency has made evident that the polity is structurally white, that the values, expectations, possibilities, are deeply bound up with the privileges of whiteness structurally understood, and those will be protected and reproduced with the full force of law's violence and pedagogical tools. The most strident among Tea Party Republicans seem desperate to hold onto that structural whiteness. So the color or race of the office holder is all but irrelevant – I stress here the "all but," the "not quite." I am tempted to say, as others have noted, that it is the *White*

House, after all. The hope invested in Obama was that he would make the White House, in George Clinton's fabulous terms, at least a bit if not a good deal more "black-brown." That imaginative re-racing of the non-racial, of the purged racial, would be to give its metaphoricity both a critical edge and a utopian reach.

America today, as I have put it elsewhere, borrowing from Alex Abramovich [2009], is as "phenomenologically fucked" racially as we've ever been. The "one drop" rule historically tried to fix in place while holding at bay the admission of the phenomenological psychoses around race. But the weight of heterogeneities has made absolutely evident to us the insane impossibility of that attempted fixity, that the reiterative necessity of the attempts to hold the conceptual and social structures in place was a fixation. Postraciality is the latest strategy to reduce the obvious to the invisible. Think in these terms of the acute ironies of a North Carolina school district's banning of Ellison's *Invisible Man* [1952] from school libraries in Randolph County because it is "not innocent, too filthy." Raciality drips off the rationalization. (In response to the enormous community pushback, the school board reversed itself a week later.)

So Obama enters the White House, the Presidency, in an impossible position. But impossibility confronts both an impropriety and a possibility, the two are brought together. He is in transgression of established histories and, as transgressor, must always make some feel uncomfortable, particularly those who already feel uncomfortable with race, many if not most white Americans no doubt, even as they say they're not. But transgression also opens up possibility, other ways of being and doing, thinking and speaking. And Obama is playing with the possibilities, in sometimes interesting ways. So he's both structurally bound by the conditions – it's impossible not to be – and tweaking them. As much as a black president colors the White House, and with it the country, the White House and the Presidency "en-lighten" its inhabitants, the First Family, after all, of color.

And then there are the structural constraints upon anybody in the position of President of the United States of America, which are enormous. We too quickly over-look those structural constraints. The President, as fig-urehead, as leader, is transformed by those structural constraints into a representative of dominant interests, in every sense of the word, despite himself.

SSG: What relationship do you see, then, between the election of Barack Obama and the emergence of the Tea Party "movement," without denying the heterogeneity of those who claim membership or affiliation? What role does race play in galvanizing its adherents? And what does the success of so many Tea Party candidates in the last couple of elections signal about the state of racial politics in the US?

DTG: The Tea Party manifested and immediately expressed itself racially after Obama's assuming office. The vocal racism at some rallies, and the enormous trash archive of racist images of the Obama family on the internet, raise the question of the Tea Party's racial index. There was certainly racial inflection in relation to the health care debate, and to Obama's election as such. If the birther movement is not racially driven and expressed, then it's hard to say what is.

This way of characterizing Obama itself speaks to a discomfort among many, particularly white, folks in America with a world long marked by global movement and America's own increasing heterogeneity. Obama's election was read by them as symbolic of the(ir) loss of America. It's symptomatic of a loss of power, of control, of presumptive privilege. It's a sense, which has been growing since the civil rights legislation, about blacks really controlling the organs of state. This emerged in some municipalities in the 1970s, to some degree at the state level in the 1990s. But now the country for these people seems to have been "taken over," and the state is no longer presumptively white "us." America has become a state of blackness. This was the final straw, at least symbolically. It didn't matter what Obama actually represented, who was in his cabinet, what forces he stood for. His election was confirmation that the burgeoning state of blackness, of non-whiteness, was now saturating political life. This extraordinary sense of loss of power, of control of state resources, of a sense of country and belonging, prompted a deep discomfort. As all these things kicked into place, wily conservative politicians recognized an opportunity in these rumblings to unsettle politics and shift them back to a capacity to create a movement, take control of it, and to put it to work on behalf of a deeply regressive slate of reactionary commitments. This was funded by once very powerful politicians like Dick Armey, and billionaires like the Koch brothers.

The anger directed by conservatives against Obama sews together concerns about losing racial standing in the society with a more vocal rejection of the Affordable Care Act or "Obamacare." The latter represents a larger rejection of the caring – the welfare – functions of the state, identified with the figure of blackness as further evidence of "being looked after" rather than self-responsible. This anger is not about to disappear. It marks an America that is much more raw, perhaps even exhausted, one likely to index anew to racial registers.

The economic is jarred today by much shorter cycles of boom and recession than has been the case until recently. This is a legacy of the past twenty or thirty years. The forces of neoliberalization effect much shorter cycles of boom and bust. In Congress, a group of conservative ideologues, committed to the undoing of the caretaking functions of government, are prepared to hasten and enlarge the bust cycles, to cause and exacerbate crisis to political and ideological ends, to the point of closing government down completely for a period. Liberated from serving the general wellbeing, they see themselves free to sabotage the economy for self-serving purposes.

The Tea Party insistence on local rule, on the conceit that it means self-determination, is really the reach to retain power in the hands of those who have long exercised it, especially white men. The vocal insistence on local rule – for immigration, schools, voting considerations, welfare rules, even taxes – invariably amounts to keeping the outsider out, to maintaining the imagined sense of purity, to restricting the benefits of belonging to those considered legitimate members of the boundaried community. Localism is a purification rite. It's the postracial way of saying "no blacks here," no one not already "us." In the US today the highest incidents of racist expression are in those areas of the country where slavery and Jim Crow segregation historically were most intense. And those are the areas also where Tea Party activity and suspicion of the federal government are most vocal.

Recourse to racism, what I will call "reiteracing," is always an expression not from confidence but from its failure. It is a failure of confidence to engage, insisting on the power of debilitation, exclusion – generically, of "put-downs" – in the face or wake of this failure. Racisms, in short, are always a defensiveness.

SSG: Given this arc of renewed racial characterization and racist expression you have drawn, can you close with thinking aloud about the sort of socialities you could imagine running outside and against the reach of the racial, as you have put it?

DTG: On that memorable night in 2008 when Obama was first elected President, there was the extraordinary picture of American – and to some considerable degree global – heterogeneity that beamed from Chicago's Grant Park. The kaleidoscope of color and culture in the park, of economic and social registers locked together, was a but fleeting image of possibility. It was to our time what Mandela's release from prison in 1991 signaled concerning the potentiality of a counter-racial sociality – or really socialities – outside the bounds if not registers of race. You could almost call this the "alter-racial" – the hints of what a genuinely nonracial sociality might look like, and aspire to.

Of course, those are also thoroughly romanticizing moments, and we are quickly brought back to earth by the push-backs to maintain homogenization, to keep out those taken not to belong, to keep in place those deemed variously unacceptable, to delimit competitiveness for resources, accessibility, and control of power. In the face of persistent delimitation, profiling, and refusal, this vision of idealized possibility must be tied to on-the-ground organization and strategic coalition-building in the perpetual commitment to struggle against racist structures, outbreaks, conceits, deceits, and denials.

I want to end, then, by briefly opening up three related considerations here. First, what should parents tell their kids about race in America? And what might youth tell their guardians, and adults generally, about racial conditions, negotiating race, and facing up to racisms? These are pressing questions not just for people of color. Racial conditions impact us all, structuring and coloring our collective sociality. What will it take collectively for youth of color not to be faced daily with social suspicion, by law enforcement and white people generally, for white youth and adults not to suspect dispositively that black folk do not readily belong in their neighborhoods and that they are up to no good? How do we become, *collectively*, socially disposed and prepared to live productively in and to contribute to increasingly heterogeneous worlds, in a society in which race no longer extends historical privilege and disprivilege, inclusion and exclusion?

Second, It has long been recognized that racisms have structured differential and unequal social and economic conditions facing differently defined and socially positioned racial groups. Insisting that racism is no more than episodic outbreaks of anomalous private individual expression, far from ending structural racism, has effectively rendered it invisible, unreachable, untouchable. The presumption of implicit racial appeal has become a central thread in the rhetorics of political dissembling and deception, as Tea Party characterizations of Obamacare bear out. Structural racism is buried, alive, behind the veil of private racist expression, innuendo, and implication. For racial neoliberalism, race evaporates, leaving racisms not bared but unrecognizable and the material inequalities prompted and extended on racial terms unidentifiable. What conceptual and analytic resources can be drawn on to recognize and effectively delimit, if not eradicate, *racisms*, structural and expressive, in the wake of *racial erasure*?

Third, there's a long tradition in the history of race-critical theory of signaling how a non-raced humanity might be fashioned out of the contrived and constrained histories of raciality. These range from Frederick Douglass's abolitionism to Sojourner Truth's assertion of black womanhood and humanity, from Anna Julia Cooper's black feminism to W.E.B. Du Bois's double consciousness, from Alain Locke's and Langston Hughes's "new Negro" to the traditions of Negritude and Black Consciousness in both the American and South African articulations, and from Frantz Fanon's humanization as a concerted push-back against the legacies of "racialization," of racially produced dehumanization, to Hannah Arendt's and Angela Davis's co-making of common worlds.

In contemporary racial considerations, the legacy of the Obama phenomenon would be to reach for a sociality drawing on these historical resources to articulate a being together, a Fanonian humanization within dynamic heterogeneities, with all their challenges and capacities.

It would be to craft together an open sociality, economically and politically, legally and culturally that recognizes the concerted contributions of all, and provides the material conditions in which everyone can express themselves, together, equitably, in raucous concert rather than stultified singularity.

Because racisms are so various and metamorphic, there are no canned solutions, no silver bullets, no pre-programmed apps. The common refrain – "so, what's *the* solution?" – is predicated on the misguided presumption that we will always be addressing the same thing, likely to respond to stereotypical interventions in predictable ways. But there is no singular "solution" because the challenges of racisms are rarely uniform, or indeed singular. More often than not they consist of a complex mix of the structural and the agentive; long-standing institutional arrangements and the attitudinal; deep-seated beliefs and flippant expressions. And no generalized principle of modern and contemporary social arrangement tends to be completely immune. I have been suggesting that broad principles of heterogeneous social commitments and equitable social standing, access, opportunity, and respect are crucial frames for countering racisms across the board. But with these at hand, each outbreak of racism, each expression, articulation, and structural surfacing will require also that it be addressed by each and all directly, concretely, specifically in the moment of its emergence and elaboration.

Antiracism, accordingly, is not just a one-time event or intervention, a feel-good moment, or referential avoidance, as with much of racelessness. It is, as Angela Davis among others always insists, a *persistence*. It requires ongoing struggle over the long haul, repeatedly having to intervene, organize, push back, reconceive, resist, invariably in light of a conception, an ideal of what socialities without and beyond racisms would amount to, look and act like. Obama gets this, perhaps from his community organizing on the streets of Chicago, but he has allowed his public political life, and not least the Presidency, to pull him back into the constraints and avoidances of racelessness, save for key moments when he has expressed himself honestly, often at the cost of inflaming conservative racialisms.

The abiding question regarding race and racisms facing us today is how to live without race while living with it, and to live with race while living without it. How do we live together, interactively, justly, without race while negotiating worlds produced and stricken by its changing terms and conditions? And how do we negotiate the existing terms of race critically, from differentiated positions of power and privilege structured historically and contemporarily by race, when its terms and effects of articulation have been rendered invisible, buried but alive?

The abiding question regarding race for our time, then, is how to be at once nonracial *and* antiracist, individually and collectively, institutionally and economically, socially and culturally. These are questions responses to which we can only fashion and materialize together.

References

Abramovich, Alex 2009. "Phenomenologically Fucked," *London Review of Books* 31, 22. 33–4.

Abu El-Haj, Nadia 2012. *The Genealogical Science: The Search for Jewish Origins and the Politics of Epistemology*. University of Chicago Press.

Alexander, Michelle 2012. *The New Jim Crow*. New Press.

Arendt, Hannah 1951. *The Origins of Totalitarianism*. Harcourt Brace Jovanovich.

Arendt, Hannah 1963. *Eichmann in Jerusalem: A Report on the Banality of Evil*. Viking.

Baldwin, James 2010. "Nationalism, Colonialism and the United States: One Minute to Twelve – A Forum." In *The Cross of Redemption: Uncollected Writings*. Ed. Randall Kenan. Pantheon.

Bauman, Zygmunt 1989. *Modernity and the Holocaust*. Cornell University Press.

Bauman, Zygmunt 2000. *Liquid Modernity*. Polity.

Beck, Ulrich 2012. *An Introduction to the Theory of Second Modernity and Risk Society*. Routledge.

Bell, Derrick 1992. *Faces at the Bottom of the Well: The Permanence of Racism*. Basic Books.

Benvenisti, Meron 2000. *Sacred Landscape: The Buried History of Palestine since 1948.* University of California Press.

Berman, Ari 2013. "7 Ways North Carolina Republicans are Trying to Make it Harder to Vote," *The Nation*, April 5. http://www.thenation.com/blog/173685/7-ways-north-carolina-republicans-are-trying-make-it-harder-vote (accessed March 6, 2014).

Blake, Mariah 2013. "George Zimmerman's Biggest Defender: A Racist with a Criminal Past," *Mother Jones*, August 8. http://www.motherjones.com/politics/2013/08/frank-taaffe-george-zimmerman-racist-white-voice (accessed March 6, 2014).

Bouie, Jamelle 2013. "Conservatives Have No Idea What 'Racist' Means," *Daily Beast*, August 7. http://www.thedailybeast.com/articles/2013/08/07/conservatives-have-no-idea-what-racist-means.html (accessed March 6, 2014).

Brown, Wendy 2006. *Regulating Aversion: Tolerance in the Age of Identity and Empire.* Princeton University Press.

Buck-Morss, Susan 2003. *Thinking Past Terror: Islamism and Critical Theory on the Left.* Norton.

Burleigh, Michael and Wippermann, Wolfgang 1991. *The Racial State: Germany 1933–1945.* Cambridge University Press.

Butler, Judith 2013. *Dispossession: The Performative in the Political.* Polity.

Callaway, Helen 1987. *Gender, Culture, and Empire: European Women in Colonial Nigeria.* University of Illinois Press.

Carter, Ben and Virdee, Satnam 2008. "Race and the Sociological Imagination," *British Journal of Sociology* 59, 4: 661–79.

Carter, Jimmy 2006. *Palestine, Peace Not Apartheid.* Simon and Schuster.

References

Carter, Stephen 1992. *Reflections of an Affirmative Action Baby*. Basic Books.

Coetzee, J.M. 1980. *Waiting for the Barbarians*. Penguin.

Cohen, G.A. 1986. "Self-Ownership, World-Ownership, and Equality." In *Justice and Equality Here and Now*. Ed. Frank S. Lucash. Cornell University Press.

Cohn, Bernard 1987. *An Anthropologist among the Historians and Other Essays*. Oxford University Press.

Comaroff, Jean and Comaroff, John L. 2001. "Millennial Capitalism: First Thoughts on a Second Coming." In *Millennial Capitalism and the Culture of Neoliberalism*. Ed. Jean Comaroff and John L. Comaroff. Duke University Press.

Crapanzano, Vincent 1985. *Waiting: The Whites of South Africa*. Random House.

Davis, Angela 1998. "Masked Racism: Reflections on the Prison Industrial Complex," ColorLines, September 10. http://colorlines.com/archives/1998/09/masked_racism_reflections_on_the_prison_industrial_complex.html (accessed March 6, 2014)

Davis, Angela 2013. "The Two Nations of Black America: Interview with Angela Davis," Frontline PBS, June 5. http://www.pbs.org/wgbh/pages/frontline/shows/race/interviews/davis.html (accessed March 6, 2014).

Derrida, Jacques 2003. "Auto-Immunity: Real and Symbolic Suicides – A Dialogue with Jacques Derrida." In *Philosophy in a Time of Terror*. Ed. Giovanna Borradori. University of Chicago Press.

Du Bois, W.E.D. 1903/1962. *The Souls of Black Folk*. Fawcett.

Ellison, Ralph 1952. *Invisible Man*. Random House.

Essed, Philomena and Goldberg, David Theo, eds, 2002. *Race Critical Theories*. Blackwell.

Fanon, Frantz 1956. *Black Skin White Masks*. Pelican.

Fanon, Frantz 1963. *The Wretched of the Earth*. Grove Weidenfeld.

References

Fanon, Frantz 1965. *A Dying Colonialism*. Grove.

Fanon, Frantz 1969. *Toward the African Revolution*. Grove.

Foucault, Michel 1970. *The Order of Things: An Archaeology of the Human Sciences*. Random House.

Foucault, Michel 1978. *History of Sexuality, Vol. I*. Pantheon.

Foucault, Michel 2003a. *Abnormal: Lectures at the Collège de France, 1974–5*. Picador.

Foucault, Michel 2003b. *Society Must Be Defended: Lectures at the Collège de France, 1975–6*. Picador.

Foucault, Michel 2008. *The Birth of Biopolitics: Lectures at the Collège de France, 1978–9*. Picador.

Foucault, Michel 2009. *Security, Territory, Population: Lectures at the Collège de France, 1977–8*. Picador.

Gates, Henry Louis and Appiah, Anthony, eds, 1992. *"Race," Writing and Difference*. University of Chicago Press.

Gilmore, Ruth Wilson 2007. *Golden Gulag: Prisons, Surplus, Crisis, and Opposition in Globalizing California*. University of California Press.

Goldberg, David Theo 1993. *Racist Culture: Philosophy and the Politics of Meaning*. Blackwell.

Goldberg, David Theo 2002a. *The Racial State*. Blackwell.

Goldberg, David Theo 2002b. "Reflections on 'Modernity, Race, and Morality." In *Race Critical Theories*. Eds Philomena Essed and David Theo Goldberg. Blackwell.

Goldberg, David Theo 2005. "(W)hacked to Pieces: Devastating America." *OpenDemocracy*, September 7. http://www.opendemocracy.net/w_hacked_to_pieces_deva_stating_america_0 (accessed March 6, 2014).

Goldberg, David Theo 2009. *The Threat of Race: Reflections on Racial Neoliberalism*. Wiley-Blackwell.

Goldberg, David Theo 2011. "Mission Accomplished: Militarizing Social Logics," *Enrique Jezik Exhibition Catalogue*. MUAC Publications (Museum of Modern Art, UNAM, Mexico City).

Habermas, Jürgen 2010. "Leadership and Leitkulture," *New York Times*, October 29. http://www.nytimes.com/2010/10/29/opinion/29Habermas.html?_r=0&pagewanted= print (accessed March 6, 2014).

Hall, Stuart 1980. "Race, Articulation, and Societies Structured in Dominance." In *Sociological Theories: Race and Colonialism*. UNESCO.

Hall, Stuart 1985. "Gramsci's Relevance to the Analysis of Racism and Ethnicity." UNESCO.

Hall, Stuart 1986. "Gramsci's Relevance for the Study of Race and Ethnicity," *Journal of Communication Inquiry* 10, 2: 5–27.

Hall, Stuart, Critcher, Chas, Jefferson, Tony, Clarke, John N., and Roberts, Brian 1978. *Policing the Crisis: Mugging, the State, and Law and Order*. Holmes and Meier.

Halsey, Margaret 1946. *Color Blind: A White Woman Looks at the Negro*. Simon and Schuster.

Hanchard, Michael 1999. "Afro-Modernity: Temporality, Politics, and the African Diaspora," *Public Culture* 11, 11: 245–68.

Harvey, David 1990. *Conditions of Postmodernity*. Blackwell.

Harvey, David 2007. *A Brief History of Neoliberalism*. Oxford University Press.

Heiner, Brady Thomas 2007. "Foucault and the Black Panthers," *City: Analysis of Urban Trends, Culture, Theory, Policy, Action* 11, 3: 313–56.

Herzl, Theodor 1896/1908. *The Jewish State*. Verlags Buchhandlung.

Hess, Moses 1861/2012. *Rome and Jerusalem: A Study in Jewish Nationalism*. Nabu Press.

Hobsbawm, Eric 1989. *The Age of Empire, 1875–1914*. Vintage.

Jaschik, Scott 2013. "Meritocracy or Bias?" *Inside Higher Ed*, August 13. http://www.insidehighered.com/news/

2013/08/13/white-definitions-merit-and-admissions-change-when-they-think-about-asian-americans (accessed March 6, 2014).

Jessop, Bob 1990. *State Theory: Putting the Capitalist State in Its Place*. Polity.

Klein, Rebecca 2013. "Hillsdale College President Arnn Under Fire for Calling Minority Students 'Dark Ones'," Huffington Post, August 1. http://www.huffingtonpost.com/2013/08/01/larry-arnn-dark-ones-hillsdale_n_3691839.html (accessed March 6, 2014).

Knafo, Saki 2013. "1 in 3 Blacks Will Go to Prison in Their Lifetime," Huffington Post, October 4. http://www.huffingtonpost.com/2013/10/04/racial-disparities-criminal-justice_n_4045144.html (accessed March 6, 2014).

Kyriakides, Christopher and Torres, Rodolfo 2012. *Race Defaced: Paradigms of Pessimism, Politics of Possibility*. Stanford University Press.

Lloyd, David and Thomas, Paul 1997. *Culture and the State*. Routledge.

Lusane, Clarence 2010. *The Black History of the White House*. City Lights Publishers.

Macey, David 2004. *Michel Foucault*. Reaktion Books.

McGeehan, Patrick 2013. "Bloomberg Calls de Blasio's Bid 'Racist'," *New York Times*, September 8. http://www.nytimes.com/2013/09/08/nyregion/bloomberg-says-de-blasio-has-run-a-racist-campaign.html?_r=0 (accessed March 6, 2014).

MacMunn, George Fletcher 1933. *The Martial Races of India*. Marston.

Maddow, Rachel 2012. *Drift: The Unmooring of American Military Power*. Broadway.

Makdisi, Saree 2010. "Apartheid/apartheid," *Salon: Johannesburg Workshop in Theory and Criticism* 2. http://jwtc.org.za/the_salon/volume_2/saree_makdisi_apartheid_apartheid.htm (accessed March 6, 2014).

Mamdani, Mahmood 2004. *Good Muslim, Bad Muslim: America, the Cold War and the Roots of Terror.* Pantheon.

Mauer, Marc and Chesney-Lind, Meda 2011. *Invisible Punishment: The Collateral Consequences of Mass Imprisonment.* New Press.

Mbembe, Achille 1992. "The Banality of Power and the Aesthetics of Vulgarity in the Postcolony," *Public Culture* 4, 2: 1–30.

Mbembe, Achille 2003. "Necropolitics," *Public Culture* 15, 1: 11–40.

Mbembe, Achille 2004. "Aesthetics of Superfluity," *Public Culture* 16, 3: 373–405.

Mda, Zakes 2002. *Ways of Dying.* Picador.

Michaels, Walter Benn 2006. *The Trouble with Diversity: How We Learned to Love Identity and Ignore Inequality.* Metropolitan Books.

Miller, James 1994. *The Passion of Michel Foucault.* Anchor.

Mitchell, W.J.T. 2012. *Seeing Through Race.* Harvard University Press.

Newfield, Christopher 2011. *Unmaking the Public University: The Forty-Year Assault on the Middle Class.* Harvard University Press.

Omi, Michael and Winant, Howard 1986. *Racial Formations in the United States: From the 1960s to the 1980s.* Routledge.

Rasmussen Reports 2013. "More Americans View Blacks as Racist Than Whites, Hispanics," *Rasmussen Reports,* July 3. http://www.rasmussenreports.com/public_content/lifestyle/general_lifestyle/july_2013/more_americans_view_blacks_as_racist_than_whites_hispanics (accessed March 6, 2014).

Reeve, Elspeth 2012. "A Conservative Conundrum: Racism Can't Kill if Racism Doesn't Exist," *The Atlantic Wire,* March 27. http://www.theatlanticwire.com/politics/2012/

03/conservatives-declare-racism-dead/50406/   (accessed March 6, 2014).

Roth, Philip 2001. *The Human Stain*. Vintage.

Rushdie, Salman 2000. *The Ground Beneath Her Feet*. Vintage.

Said, Edward 1978. *Beginnings: Intention and Method*. Pantheon.

Said, Edward 1979. *Orientalism*. Basic Books.

Slyomovics, Susan 1998. *The Object of Memory: Arab and Jew Narrate the Palestinian Village*. University of Pennsylvania Press.

Stoler, Ann 1993. *Race and the Education of Desire*. Duke University Press.

Stoler, Ann 2009. *Along the Archival Grain: Epistemic Anxieties and Colonial Common Sense*. Princeton University Press.

Thompson, Heather Ann 2013. "How Prisons Change the Balance of Power in America," *The Atlantic*, October 7. http://www.theatlantic.com/national/archive/2013/10/how-prisons-change-the-balance-of-power-in-america/280341/ (accessed March 6, 2014).

Todorov, Tzvetan 2010. *The Fear of Barbarians*. Polity.

Valayden, Chandiren 2013. *Outbreak Racism: The Embrace of Risk after Structural Racism*. Ph.D. dissertation. Theory and Culture program, University of California Irvine.

Vanhemert, Kyle 2013. "The Best Map Ever Made of America's Racial Segregation," *Wired*, August 26. http://www.wired.com/design/2013/08/how-segregated-is-your-city-this-eye-opening-map-shows-you/ (accessed March 6, 2014).

Vargas Llosa, Mario 2012. *The Dream of the Celt*. Faber and Faber.

Voegelin, Erik 1933a/1997. *Race and State* (The Collected Works, Vol. Two). University of Missouri Press.

References

Voegelin, Erik 1933b/1988. *The History of the Race Idea.* Louisiana State University Press.

Wacquant, Loïc 2002. "From Slavery to Mass Incarceration: Rethinking the 'Race Question' in the US," *New Left Review* 13, January–February. http://newleftreview.org/ II/13/loic-wacquant-from-slavery-to-mass-incarceration (accessed March 6, 2014).

Watts, Jonathan 2013. "Brazilian Funk Star Anitta Sparks New Debate about Skin Whitening and Race," *The Guardian,* September 8. http://www.theguardian.com/world/2013/sep/08/ brazilian-funk-anitta-debate-race (accessed March 6, 2014).

West, Cornel 1994. *Race Matters.* Vintage.

Wilson, Julee 2013. "Fashion Designers Accused of Racism in Letter," Huffington Post, September 6. http://www. huffingtonpost.com/2013/09/06/fashion-designers-racism-letter-bethann-hardison_n_3880363.html?utm_hp_ref= hair-beauty (accessed March 6, 2014).

Wilson, William Julius 1978. *The Declining Significance of Race: Blacks and Changing American Institutions.* University of Chicago Press.

Winant, Howard 1994. *Racial Conditions.* University of Minnesota Press.

Wing, Nick 2013. "Louie Gohmert: Obama Has Stirred Up More 'Racial Tension and Violence' Than Any President since the 1960s," Huffington Post, August 13. http:// www.huffingtonpost.com/2013/08/13/louie-gohmert-obama_n_3750116.html (accessed March 6, 2014).

Wu, Yi 2013. "Charts That Prove Prison Reform is the Most Important Economic Issue in America," *policymic.* http:// www.policymic.com/article/panelLanding?panelist_ id=5465 (accessed March 6, 2014).

Žižek, Slavoj and Goodman, Amy 2010. "Why Far Right and Xenophobic Politicians Are on the Rise in Europe," Democracy Now! Posted on October 27. http://www. alternet.org/story/148648/ (accessed March 6, 2014).

Index

About Schmidt (film), 81
Abramovich, Alex, 200
Abu El-Haj, Nadia, 85
Abu Ghraib, 126–7, 158
affirmative action, 28, 75–7,
    153–4, 165–6, 177, 188
Affordable Care Act, 202
    Obamacare, 2, 75, 190, 202,
    206
Afghanistan, 6, 10, 24, 63,
    118, 127, 184
Agamben, Giorgio, 85
Alexander, Michelle, 156
    "the new Jim Crow," 156
Althusser, Louis, 18–19, 91,
    99, 108
American Philosophy
    Association, 21
Anitta (Larissa de Macedo
    Machado), 177
antiracialism, 15, 40–1, 58,
    100, 129, 170, 171,
    173–4, 182, 207, 208
apartheid, 4, 10, 14–16, 28,
    38–40, 44, 54–5, 57,
    59–60, 64–5, 72–3, 77–8,
    102–3, 114–15, 118, 161,
    171
Arabs, 103, 184

Arendt, Hannah, 11, 41, 85,
    147, 149, 206
    banality of evil, 149
    Origins of Totalitarianism,
    11
Armey, Dick, 202
Arnn, Larry P., 177
austerity, 62, 75, 82, 120,
    152–3

Baldwin, James, 1, 3, 8–9, 13
Balibar, Étienne, 85
Banksy, 44
barbarians, 59, 121, 143, 167
Battle of Blood River, 55
Bauman, Zygmunt, 29, 30, 70,
    85
Bell, Derrick, 187
Benn, Michaels Walter, 106
Bennett, William, 167–8
Bentham, Jeremy, 27, 91
Benvenisti, Meron, 57
Berghe, Pierre van den, 47
Biko, Steve, 17
Binet, Alfred, 123
birther, 145, 195, 201
Black Consciousness, 206
Black Panthers, 86, 89
Blackwater, 116

Index

Bloomberg, Michael, 76, 180–1
borders, 6, 43, 44, 46, 139,
    141, 143, 149–50
born again racism, 171, 174,
    182
born again segregation, 78
boundaries, 5, 43–4, 47, 70,
    197, 203
Brown, Wendy, 5
Buck-Morss, Susan, 8
Burleigh, Michael, 68
Bush, George H.W., 158, 165,
    168
Bush, George W., 118, 153,
    162, 171, 194
    Bush–Cheney politics, 187
Butler, Judith, 94, 121

Calderoli, Roberto, 145
Callaway, Helen, 125
Cameron, David, 137
caretaker state, 70–6, 153, 163,
    203
Carter, Ben, 86
Carter, Jimmy, 103
Carter, Stephen, 154
Casement, Roger, 61
Chesney Lind, Meda, 162
    Invisible Punishment, 162
Chicago economists, 71
citizenship, 66, 110, 124, 131,
    133, 139, 142
Civil Rights Act, 153
Civil Rights Initiative, 28
civility, 5, 59, 81–2, 104–6,
    137
classification, 30–1, 69, 88, 103
Clinton, Bill, 153
Clinton, George, 200
Coetzee, J.M., 59
    Waiting for the Barbarians,
    59

Cohen, Gerry, 20
Cohn, Bernard, 30
color line, the, 104–5
colorblindness, 3–4, 8, 10,
    27–8, 76, 171, 173, 174,
    185
Comaroff, Jean and John L.,
    66, 94
comparativism, 47
condomization, 39, 139–40
    prophylaxis, 39
Cooper, Anna Julia, 206
Coulter, Ann, 168
Crapanzano, Vincent, 58
criminalization, 117, 133,
    153 5, 157, 158, 161,
    165, 167, 168, 180

Davis, Angela, 21, 41, 85,
    89–2, 100, 159, 180,
    206–7
de Blasio, Bill, 180
death of race, 7, 28, 35
Degler, Carl, 47
Department of Homeland
    Security, 116
Derrida, Jacques, 41–2, 44, 48,
    85, 96
    Philosophy in a Time of
    Terror, 41
    Writing and Difference, 21
diversity, 6, 25, 131–2, 177,
    186
Douglass, Frederick, 206
Du Bois, W.E.B., 40, 67,
    104–7, 206
    The Souls of Black Folk, 104
Duggan, Mark, 177

Eisenhower, Dwight D., 111
Elizabeth City State University,
    164

Ellison, Ralph, 200
  Invisible Man, 200
England, Lynndie, 126–7
Essed, Philomena, 46

Fanon, Frantz, 18, 41, 85, 105,
  174, 181, 206
  Black Skin White Masks, 18
  A Dying Colonialism, 18
  *Toward the African
    Revolution*, 18
  Wretched of the Earth, 18
felony, 161–3, 179
FEMA, 79, 163
financialization, 73–4, 120,
  152, 190
food stamps, 75, 163, 192
Fortuyn, Pim, 136
Foucault, Michel, v, 19–20, 49,
  71, 78, 80, 83–107, 113
  Abnormal, 89
  "The Birth of Biopolitics,"
    71
  Discipline and Punish, 91
  *The Government of Self and
    Others*, 89
  The History of Sexuality, 97
  Madness and Civilization, 90
  The Order of Things, 90–1,
    101
  *Security, Territory,
    Population*, 89
  Society Must Be Defended,
    83, 88–9, 96–7, 105
France, Anatole, 146
Frankfurt school, 67

Gates, Henry Louis (Skip), 21,
  183, 195–6
Genet, Jean, 92
Gilmore, Ruth Wilson, 34
Gilroy, Paul, 16, 85

Goldberg, David Theo, 2
  "Mission Accomplished:
    Militarizing Social Logics,"
    78
  The Racial State, 22–3,
    26, 35, 67–9, 92–3, 108,
    125
  Racist Culture, 14, 20, 26,
    78–9, 85, 92, 97
  The Threat of Race, 7, 11,
    35, 41, 78, 96, 108
Gordon, Lewis, 174
governmentality, 30, 52, 70,
  72, 89, 92–3, 100, 110,
  154, 161
Gramsci, Antonio, 19, 91–2
  The Prison Notebooks, 91
Groupe d'Information sur les
  Prisons, 90
Guantánamo Bay, 6, 147, 184

Habermas, Jürgen, 130, 135,
  137
Haider, Jörg, 136
Hall, Stuart, ii, 21, 41, 70, 83,
  85, 92
  "Gramsci's Relevance to the
    Analysis of Racism and
    Ethnicity," 92
  Policing the Crisis, 21, 133
  *Societies Structured in
    Dominance*, 21
Halsey, Margaret, 28
  Color Blind, 28
Hanchard, Michael, 58
Hardison, Bethann, 176
Harlan, John Marshall, 27
Harvey, David, 70,
  *A Brief History of
    Neoliberalism*, 71
  Condition of Postmodernity,
    70

Index

Heiner, Brady, 86, 89–92, 105
  "Foucault and the Black
  Panthers," 86
Heritage Foundation, 182
Herzl, Theodor, 103
  The Jewish State, 103
Hess, Moses, 102-103
heterogeneity, 9, 12, 25, 29–33,
  41–2, 45–6, 53, 75–6, 80,
  95, 134–5, 160, 166, 186,
  200–2, 204–7
higher education, 12, 157
Hillsdale College, 177
Hirschfeld, Magnus, 41, 67
Hobbes, Thomas, 20, 22, 27
Hobsbawm, Eric, 99
Holocaust, 57, 103, 135
homogeneity, 8, 29–33, 41, 45,
  76, 78, 95, 102, 131, 166,
  204
Horton, Willie, 168, 181
Hughes, Langston, 206

imaginative geographies, 21,
  122
Iman, 176
immigration, vi, 47, 66, 75–6,
  130–3, 136–7, 139,
  145, 148, 150 186, 195,
  203
incarceration, 4, 17, 153–6,
  162, 166, 175, 195
individualization, 5, 31, 73–4,
  113, 115, 124, 163, 166,
  175, 190–1, 194
IQ testing, 123
Iraq, 6, 10, 24–5, 63, 115–16,
  118, 120, 126–7
Israel, 10, 22, 41, 43, 53,
  57, 59, 103, 106, 118,
  121, 126–7, 134, 144,
  148–9

Jackson, George, 86, 89,
  90–2
Jackson, Jesse, 63
Jessop, Bob, 69
Jim Crow, 115, 156, 160, 162,
  181, 203
Jones, Terry, 184

Kant, Immanuel, 27, 90
Katrina (Hurricane), 29, 79–80,
  82, 109, 115–16, 163
Kennedy, Bobby, 1
King, Martin Luther, 105
King, Steve, 102
Knox, Robert, 40
Koch Brothers, 202
Kyenge, Cécile, 145
Kyriakides, Christopher, 86,
  93, 100 1
  Race Defaced, 86

Landrieu, Mitch, 80
latinamericanization, 33, 38
Lawson, Bill, 21
Legassick, Martin, 19
liberalism, 16, 20, 26, 28, 31
Liberation Committee for
  Africa, 1
Limbaugh, Rush, 168
liquid modernity, 70
Lloyd, David, 68
  Culture and the State, 68
Locke, Alain, 206
Locke, John, 27, 31
logic of militarization, 114,
  141
Lott, Tommy, 21
Loving v. Virginia, 176
Lusane, Clarence, 196
  The Black History of the
  White House, 196
  The Butler, 196

Index

Macey, David, 91
McGary, Howard, 21
McGeehan, Patrick, 181
MacMunn, George Fletcher, 123
Maddow, Rachel, 128
Madrid bombings, 135
Magubane, Ben, 19
Makdisi, Saree, 57, 103
make-believe, 26, 57, 78, 90, 144
Mamdani, Mahmood, 5
Mandela, Nelson, 17, 204
martial races, 123–4
Martin, Trayvon, 6, 25, 29, 34, 54, 64, 178, 179, 180–3, 195
Marx, Karl, 19–20, 47, 86, 100
Mauer, Marc, 162
  Invisible Punishment, 162
Mbembe, Achille, 2, 23, 49, 83, 85, 160
Mda, Zakes, 61
  Ways of Dying, 61
Merkel, Angela, 130, 137
messianism, 50, 54, 58, 64–5, 172
Mexico, 6, 44, 141–3, 148, 192
migration, v, 40, 130–51
militarization, 22, 44, 106, 108–14, 116, 117, 119–21, 122, 124, 125, 127–8, 130, 139, 144, 158–9
militarizing society, v, 108–29, 159, 161
military-industrial complex, 73–4, 111
millennialism, 35–6, 65, 135, 171
Miller, James, 89

Mitchell, Tom, 174
MSNBC, 81
multiculturalism, 6, 8, 130, 132–5, 137, 173, 186
Muslim Brotherhood, 99

Nagin, Ray, 80
National Rifle Association, 141
necropolitics, 23, 34, 160
Negritude, 206
neoconservatism, 2, 71
neoliberalism, 3–6, 28, 71, 72, 74–5, 80–2, 108, 114–15, 117, 119, 132, 152, 153, 156, 163, 167, 175, 188–92, 203, 206
neoneoliberalism, 188
New Orleans, 78–80, 115–17, 174
New York Society for Black Philosophy, 21
Newfield, Christopher, 12
Nietzsche, Friedrich, 90
  Genealogy of Morals, 90
Nixon, Richard, 168
No Child Left Behind, 164
nonracial, 9, 170–3, 178, 198, 200, 204, 208
Norquist, Grover, 74–5
NYPD, 157

O'Mara, Mark, 180
O'Reilly, Bill, 179
Obama, Barack, v, 3–4, 62–4, 118, 144, 154, 168, 180–208
Obama, Michelle, 63
Omi, Michael, 21, 68
  Racial Formations, 21, 68
Operation Enduring Freedom, 81
Outlaw, Lucius, 21

Index

Pakistan, 43, 63, 134
Palestine, 6, 10, 24–5, 43–4,
    57, 103, 106, 118, 134,
    144
palestinianization, 35, 38
    racial palestinianization, 22,
    102
participatory individualism, 190
permanent war, 25, 104–5
Plessy v. Ferguson, 27
political theology of race,
    10–11, 48–50, 55, 64
polygenism, 50–1
postracial raciology, 118
postracialism, 7–9, 27, 129,
    170–1, 178–9, 181–6, 191,
    193, 196, 198, 200, 203
Powell, Enoch, 102, 132
    "Rivers of Blood" (speech),
    132
Prettyman, Al, 21
Prince, Erik, 116
prison industrial complex, 154
privatization, 5, 28–9, 32–3,
    73–4, 77, 80, 82, 116–17,
    152, 166, 168, 190–1
purity, 96, 101–3, 172, 203

race critical theory, 46
race war, 88–9, 97–9, 105
racelessness, 4, 11, 22, 25–6,
    28–9, 35–6, 38, 52, 74,
    76, 122, 173–4, 183,
    207–8
racial americanization, 22, 35,
    38–9, 78
racial duress, 191–3
racial evacuation, 52
racial historicism, 22–3, 127
Racial Privacy Act, 28, 168
racial profiling, 112, 147, 157,
    179, 183

racial regionalizations, 37, 40
racial reversibility, 179–80, 185
racialization, 35–7, 105, 206
raciologics, v, 108–29, 179,
    184
Rasmussen Reports, 179
Reagan, Ronald, 14, 28, 71,
    153, 165, 168, 187
Reeve, Elspeth, 182
regime of truth, 26, 49, 109,
    119, 121, 127
Reid, Harry, 193
Reynolds, William Bradford,
    165
Rice, Condoleezza, 126
Riehl, Dan, 180
Romney, Mitt, 24, 112, 139,
    144, 179
Roth, Phillp, 102
Rousseau, Jean-Jacques, 27
Rushdie, Salman, 173
    *The Ground Beneath Her
    Feet*, 173
Ryan, Paul, 24

Said, Edward, 19
    Orientalism, 19, 21
Sandberg, Sheryl, 128
self-strangulating society, 7–8,
    41–2, 156
Sheehan, Cindy, 128
Slyomovics, Susan, 57
social death, 162, 169
social regulation, 115, 152,
    190
South Africa, 4, 11, 14–19, 28,
    36, 38–40, 44, 47, 49–50,
    54, 56, 58–9, 73, 77,
    118–19, 128, 158, 161,
    173, 186
    Afrikaners, 59, 64
    Robben Island, 17

southernafricanization, 35
Starkey, David, 177
Steele, Shelby, 167–8
Stoler, Ann, 83, 85, 96–7
    Along the Archival Grain,
    97
    *Race and the Education of
    Desire*, 83, 96–7
stop and frisk, 76, 112, 157,
    180, 183
structural racism, 205–6
subjectification, 93–4
subjectivation, 93–5
suburbanization, 155

Tea Party, 137–9, 149, 188,
    193, 195, 199, 201,
    203–4, 206
Thatcher, Margaret, 28, 71
Thatcherites, 102
Thomas, Paul, 68
    Culture and the State, 68
thoughtlessness, 147–50
threat, 3, 7, 41, 115, 133, 140,
    147, 192
Todorov, Tzvetan 143
Torres, Rodolfo, 86, 93, 100–1
    Race Defaced, 86
transcendent critique, 100
Truth, Sojourner, 206
Truth and Reconciliation
    Commission, 55
Tutu, Desmond, 55

UNESCO, 92
universal health care, 160

Valayden, Chandiren, 87, 190
Vargas Llosa, Mario, 61
Verdonk, Rita, 136
video games, 111, 121–2

Virdee, Satnam, 86
Voegelin, Eric, 41, 49, 67–8
    *The History of the Race
    Idea*, 67
von Spakovsky, Hans, 182
von Trier, Lars, 65
    Melancholia, 65
Voortrekker Monument, 55
Voting Rights Act, 28, 154,
    164
Voto Latino, 128

Wacquant, Loïc, 160–1
Wallace, George, 177
walls, 52, 139–41, 150
Walsh, Joe, 168
weight of race, 58–61
welfarism, 3, 61, 70–1, 74–6,
    82, 136, 153, 163, 192,
    203
West, Cornel, 21, 128
whiteness, 33–4, 77, 96, 125,
    134, 176, 199, 202
Wilders, Geert, 53, 136
Wilson, Gilmore Ruth, 34,
Wilson, William Julius, 106
    *Declining Significance of
    Race*, 106
Winant, Howard, 21, 36, 68
    Racial Formations, 68
Wippermann, Wolfgang, 68
Wolpe, Harold, 19
World War II, 24, 27–8, 38,
    41, 70, 109, 131, 136,
    142, 171

Zimmerman, George, 25, 29,
    54, 178–82
Zionism, 102
Žižek, Slavoj, 130–1, 135,
    137–8